· T E N ·
V I N E Y A R D
L U N C H E S

RICHARD OLNEY

· TEN ·
VINEYARD
LUNCHES

EBURY PRESS
LONDON

Published by Ebury Press
Division of the National Magazine Company Ltd
Colquhoun House
27–37 Broadwick Street
London W1V 1FR

First impression 1988

Designed and produced by
Sheldrake Press Ltd
188 Cavendish Road
London SW12 ODA

EDITOR: SIMON RIGGE
Managing Editor: Eleanor Lines
Art Direction and Book Design: Ivor Claydon, Bob Hook
Photography: Bob Komar assisted by Kim Golding
Artwork: Sarah McMenemy
Assistant Editors: Tim Fraser, Vicky Hayward
Sub-Editor: Norma Macmillan
Editorial Assistant: Joan Lee

Printed in Italy by Imago Publishing
ISBN 0 85223 606 9

THE AUTHOR

Richard Olney is one of America's foremost cooks and a member of the
Académie Internationale du Vin. While pursuing his career as an artist, he
began writing about food and wine when he took up residence in France in
1951; he is the author of numerous articles for magazines and journals and
has been a regular contributor to *Cuisine et Vins de France*. He was chief
consultant to the Time-Life *Good Cook* series, and has written a number of
highly regarded books, including the *French Menu Cookbook* (1970), *Simple
French Food* (1974), and *Yquem*, a history of the wine of
Château d'Yquem (1986).

CONTENTS

Introduction	6
Aromatics and Basic Preparations	13
Basic Recipes and Techniques	18
Mirepoix	18
Little Stocks	18
Basic Sausage Meat	19
To Turn Artichokes	20
To Peel (or Blanch) Almonds and Pistachios	20
Pastry	20
Sabayon Sauce	21
Raspberry Sauce	21
Map of the Wine Regions of France	22

CHAPTER ONE PAGE 24
SUBTLETIES OF NORTHERN BURGUNDY

Scrambled Eggs with Asparagus	28
Roast Beef	30
Braised Artichoke Bottoms with Glazed Onions	31
Honey Ice Cream with Raspberry Sauce	33

CHAPTER TWO PAGE 34
THE AUTUMN TABLE OF SOUTHERN BURGUNDY

Stuffed Onions Baked in Cream Sauce	38
Truffled Sausage with Pistachios in Court-Bouillon, New Potatoes in their Skins	40
Pig's Trotters and Cabbage Braised in Beaujolais	42
Macedoine of Fruits in Beaujolais	43

CHAPTER THREE PAGE 44
RICHES OF THE NORTHERN COTES DU RHONE

Seafood Salad with Saffron Cream Sauce	48
Stuffed, Braised Lamb Shoulder	50
White Purée	52
Peaches in Red Crozes-Hermitage	53

CHAPTER FOUR PAGE 54
THE SOUTHERN COTES DU RHONE AND PROVENCE

Courgette and Tomato Tart	59
Brochettes of Lamb Parts in Caul	60
Pilaf with Spring Vegetables	61
Gratin of Fresh Figs	63

CHAPTER FIVE PAGE 64
ROBUST SIMPLICITY FROM THE SOUTH WEST

Braised Chicory	68
Oxtail and Pig's Ear Stew	70
Honey-Glazed Apple Tart	72

CHAPTER SIX PAGE 74
FLAVOURS OF SOUTHERN BORDEAUX

Oysters and Green Sausages	80
Veal Sweetbreads Sweated in Sauternes	82
Leg of Lamb on a Bed of Potatoes	82
Green Beans	83
Almond Bavarian Cream and Peaches in Sauternes	84

CHAPTER SEVEN PAGE 86
CLASSICS OF NORTHERN BORDEAUX

Duck Terrine	92
Brochettes of Scallops, Monkfish and Bacon	94
Roast Pheasant	96
Potato Straw Cake	98
Pear and Red Wine Ice	98

CHAPTER EIGHT PAGE 100
DEPTH AND DELICACY FROM THE LOIRE

Stuffed Braised Squid Smothered in Little Peas	106
Roast Pork Loin Stuffed with Apricots	107
Turnip Gratin	108
Baked Pears	109

CHAPTER NINE PAGE 110
TASTES OF THE JURA

Stuffed Courgette Flowers	113
Braised Stuffed Duck with Olives	114
Souffléed Crêpes with Almonds and Sabayon Sauce	118

CHAPTER TEN PAGE 120
THE ELEGANCE OF ALSACE

Persillade of Sole and Sliced Artichokes	123
Baked Rabbit in Saffron Cream	124
Fresh Noodles	125
Peach and Bread Pudding with Sabayon Sauce	126

Introduction

Every meal is a celebration. My daily meals, celebrated for the most part in solitude, sometimes with family or *à l'improviste* with friends who turn up with little advance notice, are those which I hold most dear.

The most wonderful are those of the summer months; the quality of the light and the air of Provence, scented with the same essences that have condimented the vinegar and the salads, are as vital as the coolness of the wine and the food itself. At the dinner hour the terrace, laced with coloured lights, is transformed into a funny little theatre with a vaguely carnival atmosphere.

For these meals, I have no need to think about what goes with what. My daily white and rosé wines accompany perfectly the luncheon salads and the dinner starter, as often as not a hot, parboiled vegetable – green beans, asparagus, cauliflower, broccoli, chard, etc. – anointed with olive oil and lemon or vinegar at table; a red Bandol or a Chinon goes equally well with meats from my fireplace grill – or the pot-pourri of leftovers in the form of ragoût, daube, pilaf, gratin or whatnot – and the cheeses that make up the body of the evening meal.

In season, I can ill support a day without a tomato salad at one meal or the other. It is always the same – thinly sliced tomatoes fanned out on a platter, sliced green onions or onion rings, coarse sea salt and pepper ground over, dribbled with olive oil, a few drops of my herb vinegar, without which I would be helpless, and an abundant scattering of torn-up basil leaves and flower buds. (I once received a lady restaurateur from the Deep South who watched my every move in the kitchen and, as I began to slice the tomatoes, said, 'Honey, you better peel those tomatoes or I might get some skin stuck in my teeth!' I bowed to the lady's wishes but the salad was none the better for it.)

This tomato salad is often one of several, grilled red

and yellow peppers being another favourite. The peppers are grilled until semi-cooked, the flesh soft, the skins regularly blistered and irregularly charred, then placed on a platter and enclosed in a plastic bag until tepid before being peeled and seeded. The steam trapped in the bag loosens the skins, which slip off easily, and the juices that flow on to the platter are a precious addition to the vinaigrette.

When they are not spread out on a platter with a garlicky vinaigrette spooned over, the peppers are torn into strips and thrown into the bottom of a salad bowl with onion rings, to macerate in vinaigrette, the salad servers crossed above them to keep the vinaigrette out of contact with the other elements: a variety of green, leafy things – including basil and bitter, peppery greens – and green beans, parboiled, drained, cooled till tepid (not refreshed) and tossed atop. Garnishing the salad are sections of tomato and hard-boiled egg – a manner of speaking, for the eggs are neither hard nor boiled. Covered with cold water, brought very slowly to a near simmer, then held for a few minutes over very low heat before being refreshed in cold water, they have tender instead of rubbery whites and yolks moist at the heart. When hyssop is in bloom, its ultramarine flowers are scattered over the eggs and finely chopped hyssop leaves over the rest; nasturtium blossoms often lend their peppery flavour and flashes of hot colour.

This salad, or variations thereupon, often with avocado wedges or leftover vegetables, pulses, rice, pasta or slivered meats replacing the peppers in the maceration, adorns my luncheon table more often than any other single preparation (the tomato salad is then moved to the evening starter). I know of nothing more beautiful than the out-of-doors summer light playing across its surface. Of course, it must be tossed at table only at the moment of serving – and tossed thoroughly and repeatedly.

Salads often depend on what leftovers are lying in wait. Take the example of the squid and souffléed crêpes in this book. It is well worth preparing too much of both to profit from in the next day's salad: a feast of stuffed squid slices garnished with crêpes – rolled up and cut, like noodles, into ribbons – and other odds and ends, lightly seasoned and dribbled with olive oil and vinegar. The tender-textured, sweet-flavoured ribbons provide a lovely garnish to any number of salads, soups or stews.

Another category of meal, which falls perhaps every

week or ten days into the pattern of my life, results from friends, aware that I don't drive and that I hate going down the hillside, ringing up to suggest that they shop and come to dinner. Although these meals are moistened by a more varied selection of wines (only old, sedimented bottles that require being stood up a day or two in advance of decanting being out of bounds) the wines cannot be chosen until the shopping basket has arrived, its contents unveiled and a menu conceived. It is on these occasions that invention, not only in the kitchen but in the pairing of foods and wines, is given the freest rein – and that, sometimes, unexpectedly successful marriages are discovered. As to the food, if it is remembered in spirit, it is forgotten in detail, for I never take notes, on the (until now) mistaken assumption that I will never write another cookery book... and with the certain knowledge that I will never prepare anything twice the same way, in any case.

When I organise a menu in advance – a rarity these days – I like to choose the wines first (typically, for a menu limited to first course, main course, cheese and dessert these will be Champagne for apéritif, a white wine

A tossed-together salad, garnished with boiled eggs

to open the meal, two red wines from the same region or of a similar style, and a Sauternes). The choice of wines depends very much on who my guests are to be; winemakers are nearly always amongst them and I try to choose wines that they are not likely to be able to drink often. Only when I have settled on the specific wines do I begin to think about the foods and the details of the preparations that are to accompany them (this is also the way that I prefer to order a restaurant meal – clashes of will have more than once disturbed the serenity of a starspangled table when an old-fashioned *maître d'hôtel* has refused to send around the wine steward before taking the order).

The formula of this book is based on this concept of a menu also – necessarily, in order to present within a restrained context as many wines as possible from the different French viticultural regions. But it is my prayer that readers will not take the formula too seriously; the *raison d'être* of the table, after all, is to have a good time. If everyone, guest and host alike, is not relaxed and happy, the meal is a failure, no matter how perfect the food and the wine.

There is nothing formal about my table – unless an array of wine glasses be considered formal – and, because I am most comfortable dressed in rags, that is the way I receive. My main concern is that everyone fall immediately into a relaxed atmosphere. As the kitchen is the largest room in the house and meals are served there, before the fireplace, when the weather does not permit eating on the terrace, it is also a combined centre of cooking and social activity during the often extended apéritif hour.

I don't much worry about timing – as long as the Champagne glasses are kept filled no one minds lingering before going to table – but I am careful to finish tedious tasks before anyone's arrival, for guests seem always to take special pleasure in watching me at work; in unspoken complicity, I save the bits of theatre, sleights-of-hand, foods being tossed in the air over leaping flames, decanting and whatnot for their participation.

Since I do not like surprises or blind tastings at table and assume that my guests share this aversion, each receives a card upon which is scribbled the menu and the accompanying wines. I pamper the wines, often refrigerating decanted red wines for half an hour lest they approach the infamous 'room temperature', and pour each wine before its accompanying course is served for, however successful the alliance, those who are passionate about wine always want to taste it first with nothing but a nibble of bread.

A sidelight to these meals is invariably a visit to the cellar. I am proud of it in the child-like way that one is of anything hewn and fashioned with one's own hands. Each time I am surprised and delighted anew at the admiration it elicits from vignerons, though it is impressive, not for its size but for the relatively constant cool temperature and humidity, qualities owing much to the property having once been a limestone quarry.

Perhaps I owe an apology to the Champenois for not including a Champagne chapter here but, under most circumstances, the genius of Champagne seems to me best expressed at the apéritif hour. It is, moreover, difficult, outside Champagne itself, to procure a series sufficiently different in character – ranging from fresh, youngish *blanc de blancs* to old, but recently disgorged, assemblages containing a high proportion of Pinot noir – to create an exciting progression on a menu. Champagne is the best place to experience an all-Champagne menu; Gérard Boyer's cellar at Les Crayères in Reims is unequalled in its choice, as is his talent for matching his culinary creations to different Champagnes.

FRENCH WINE CLASSIFICATIONS

Brief explanations of official classifications occur in some of the chapter introductions to follow. The classifications of the Côte d'Or, in Burgundy, and of the principal regions of Bordeaux are insular; if considered separately, each may seem to make sense but, taken together, they become very confusing. The Appellation d'Origine Controlée (A.O.C.), as defined by the Institut National des Appellations d'Origine (I.N.A.O.), in some instances incorporates the terms of the regional classification into the *appellation contrôlée*; in others it does not. By some miracle, all of the classifications use the same vocabulary but the words do not have the same meanings; Grand and Premier assume different levels of distinction in each classification (when the word 'Grand' does not occur in the official classification, as in Médoc where the highest distinction is Premier Cru, its use is not controlled and it appears indiscriminately on labels) and a *cru* (growth) in Burgundy bears no relation to a *cru* in Bordeaux.

The Côte d'Or appellations, Grand Cru and Premier

Cru, are merely a consecration, as defined by centuries of tradition and officialised by the I.N.A.O., of the place-names associated with the specific soils and micro-climates (usually minuscule and nearly always shared by a number of proprietors) which produce the greatest and the next-greatest wines of Burgundy.

In Bordeaux, a *cru* is a privately owned or company-owned estate, often vast and encompassing a variety of soils and micro-climates, rather than a minute circum-scription of soil and micro-climate. The different Bor-deaux classifications, with a century and more separating those of Médoc and Sauternes (1855) from Saint-Emilion (1955) and Graves (1959), were formulated under differ-ent circumstances and for different reasons.

The 1985 revision of the Saint-Emilion classification lists eleven Premiers Grands Crus Classés, with Ausone and Cheval Blanc heading the list (previously these two were listed as category A and the others as category B), and something over 60 Grands Crus Classés. The I.N.A.O. sanctions the inclusion of these classifications, following the words Saint-Emilion, in the A.O.C. (i.e., 'Château Figeac, Appellation Saint-Emilion Premier Grand Cru Classé Contrôlée'), whereas the Sauternes, Graves and Médoc A.O.C.s, despite their official classifi-cations, are only generic, whether regional or village (i.e., 'Château Haut-Brion, Appellation Graves Contrôlée'; 'Château Lafite-Rothschild, Appellation Pauillac Contrôlée').

Before presenting the wines of Bordeaux at the Paris World Fair in 1855, the Bordeaux Chamber of Com-merce requested the Bordeaux Syndicate of Wine Brokers to prepare separate classifications of 'The White Wines of the Gironde' (discussed in Chapter 6) and 'The Red Wines of the Gironde'. With the exception of one Graves – Château Haut-Brion – the red wines were all Médocs, 57 in all, separated into first, second, third, fourth and fifth growths according to the prices they fetched. The first growths, or Premiers Crus, were Châteaux Lafite, Latour, Margaux and Haut-Brion. Except for the disappearance of a couple of properties, the splitting of a few others and Mouton's ascension, in 1972, from second to first growth, that classification remains unaltered and official. (In addition to the 1855 classifica-tion, a classification of 120 or so 'unclassified' Médoc growths, broken down into three categories, Crus Grands Bourgeois Exceptionnels, Crus Grands Bourgeois and Crus Bourgeois, has most recently been reformulated in 1978.)

The wines of Pomerol have never been officially classified. Médoc's Premiers Crus, then, are the equivalents, in terms of prestige, to Sauternes' Premier Cru Supérieur (Yquem), to a half dozen of the Côte d'Or's Grands Crus (Romanée Conti, Montrachet, La Tâche, Chambertin Clos de Bèze...), to Saint-Emilion's first two Premiers Grands Crus Classés and to Pomerol's unclassified Château Pétrus.

WINE SERVICE

I have never decanted a bottle of white wine and rarely decanted a red wine less than eight or ten years old (although sometimes a splashy passage from bottle to decanter will open up a young wine more rapidly). Because, when old, they are often fragile and susceptible to oxidation, I prefer never to decant Burgundies. Sedimented bottles of other red wines should, ideally, be stood upright in the cellar a day or two before decanting so that all loose sediment slides gently into the punt. The bottle should be moved and uncorked, upright and without jiggling, after first cutting beneath the neck ridge to remove the top of the capsule and cleaning the top of the neck and cork with a cloth or paper towel, dampened if necessary; after uncorking, the neck end should again be wiped clean, inside and out. Holding the bottle from the side that faced up when laid down, pour steadily and slowly until the glug-glugging stops and the wine flows silently, then pour more rapidly, moving the neck of the bottle over a tiny light source, candle flame or other, and stopping abruptly as soon as the first sign of sediment appears.

Controversy concerning wine temperatures is silly. All wine should give the impression of coolness when drunk. No doubt every wine has its ideal temperature, which may vary with the seasons and with its stage of evolution: younger wines are best drunk cooler than older wines; wines that are not expected to improve with age are best drunk cooler than wines with a future; red Burgundies are probably best drunk cooler than red Bordeaux; most white wines are best drunk cooler than most red wines.... Personal preference plays a certain role but less, I think, than one imagines.

I figure that no wine should be served colder than

about 6°–8°C (45°F) or warmer than about 16°C (60°F), the lower temperature is fine for a Muscadet or an Entre-Deux-Mers but would paralyse a Montrachet; the higher temperature is fine for an Hermitage but would shatter a Beaujolais. Most white wines are served too cold and most red wines too warm – and it is rare that the latter are served at less than 20°–22°C (70°F)! It is a mistake to freeze such a variable and seductive landscape with rigid rules, but it is important always to be aware of temperature. If a wine seems to lack something, it may be simply that it is too cool or too warm; don't hesitate to remove a white wine from its ice bucket if its bouquet is disappearing or to plunge a red wine into a bucket if it lacks freshness and its alcohol is evident.

Many a wine has been damaged or destroyed by the stale odour of a wine glass; more often than not, the fault is unfairly put down to the wine. The best kept of cupboards always harbour odours; wine glasses stored upside-down always gather stale odours. Unless your glasses are used daily and stored standing up, they should be rinsed in hot water and dried with a clean, dry, lintless towel before being used; in any case, they should always be smelled before being used. If the glasses have been recently washed and the odour is barely perceptible, it will usually disappear if the glasses are simply polished with a dry towel. The touch and the taste of glasses that have been washed in a dishwasher are also troubling and increasingly prevalent.

AROMATICS AND BASIC PREPARATIONS

Salt and Pepper

My kitchen contains no fine salt. I use two coarse sea salts, one grey, the other 'refined' (white). The grey salt has the finest flavour but it holds too much moisture to be used in a salt grinder and it throws quite a heavy scum, harmless but unattractive, when added to boiling water. The white salt is reserved for anything that requires seasoning with finely ground salt, for boiling vegetables and for use at the table.

I use a mixture of approximately five parts of black pepper and three parts of white pepper to one of allspice in my pepper grinders. Because of the uneven sizes of the allspice berries, the larger ones must be coarsely broken up in a mortar before being added to the mixture. The omission of pepper in many of the recipes to follow is not an oversight: cooked in a liquid medium, pepper turns bitter and loses the aromatic qualities that are its chief virtues. I never use it in soups, stews, stocks, sauces or in gratins which begin cooking in liquid; I always use it in stuffings, terrines, sausages and pâtés, and often for seasoning meats interiorly or for roasting and grilling. The pepper grinder is always at table and is meant to be used.

Herbs
Thyme, rosemary, oregano, winter savory, fennel and bay grow in wild profusion on the Provençal hillsides (locally, thyme takes the pretty name of *farigoulette* and winter savory is *pebre d'ase* – 'ass's pepper'). Wild in the garden are borage, burnet and purslane, the latter a garden pest but a welcome addition to salads; the cultivated herbs I grow are marjoram, hyssop, basil, sage, lovage, flat-leafed parsley, chives, tarragon, rocket, sorrel, mint, lemon balm, lemon thyme and serpolet thyme. Fresh coriander has been abandoned because of its antipathy to wine; dill and chervil do not adapt to the climate or the soil.

Mixed dried herbs: thyme comes into flower in April and oregano in July; cultivated marjoram is in flower bud and flowering throughout the summer and winter savory begins to flower at the end of July. It is at these times that the four herbs which make up my dried herb mixture are collected, the branches gathered into bouquets, tied and hung upside-down, over the fireplace and from rafters throughout the house, until dried. After a couple of weeks, they are packed into large paper bags (recovered from American supermarkets – France has swept definitively into the age of plastic) with other paper bags pulled over the open tops, permitting, at the same time, aeration and protection from dust. Except for a few bouquets of oregano, saved for use alone throughout the year, all the herbs are assembled in the autumn, the bouquets crumbled between gloved hands, the crumbs passed in an electric processor, sieved to remove branch fragments and packed into glass jars for storage in an unheated, unlighted room. I am not particular about specific proportions but thyme always dominates, followed by oregano, marjoram and savory, in descending proportions. The semi-stripped bouquets are saved for steeping in vinegar, others being tossed occasionally into the fireplace to flavour grilled foods or to scent the air.

Parsley: flat-leafed or common parsley, if freshly picked, has a firm and individual taste that will surprise anyone accustomed to the coarse and banal curly variety. Parsley is biennial but it must be planted every year for a regular supply because it bolts, flowers and seeds in the second year. The second-year plants, however, should be torn up only as needed in the kitchen, for the roots are intensely aromatic, a far more valuable addition to bouquets garnis or for tossing loosely into stews, stocks and courts-bouillons than the parsley stems usually recommended in their absence.

If the parsley is picked in an insecticide-free garden, don't wash it. In any case, to chop it finely and cleanly, the leaves must retain no trace of humidity and the chopping knife should be large and very sharp. A stalk of parsley branches into three stems terminating in leaves. Tear the longer, central stems off where they branch from the stalks and pull all the stems between thumb and forefinger into a bouquet pinched tightly at the base of the leaves; fold the leaves under to form a compact mass, held together by fingertips, and slice it into fine threads, guiding the knife-blade with slightly in-turned finger-tips. Once through is all that is necessary – the result is absolutely dry, light and feathery.

Persillade: a persillade is a mixture of garlic and chopped parsley. It can be prepared in two ways, depending on its use. For incorporation into stuffings and other mixtures before cooking, I prefer to pound the garlic, with a pinch of coarse salt, to a paste in a mortar before mixing in the parsley, chopped as described above; this produces a sticky persillade which disperses unevenly when used as a last-minute addition to rapid sautés. For these, I chop the garlic finely, first slicing it into paper-thin slices, then chopping through it repeatedly, before tossing it lightly with the parsley. One clove of garlic and two or three tablespoons of finely chopped parsley will do for any of the recipes in this book.

Vinegar and Aromatic Vinegar

My *vinaigrier* is a 15 litre (3 gallon) oak cask, permanently furnished with a long-necked glass funnel held in place by a cork at the bung-hole, a spigot and, bored at the top of the same face as the spigot, a hole for aeration. A film of plastic pressed over the funnel keeps out the dust; muslin, tacked over the aeration hole, keeps out the midges. The wine contained between the level of the spigot and that of

Assembling a red wine marinade
for oxtail pieces (recipe page 70)

the aeration hole is 10 litres of 14 bottles. After ten months or so the finished vinegar, approximately one-third of which will have evaporated, is drawn off to the spigot level into a stoneware jug; in the jug have been placed bundles of dried herbs (see above) plus a few bay leaves, a couple of branches each of rosemary and sage and a handful of bruised but unpeeled garlic cloves. The jug is then covered with a plate and left for a month or so before the aromatic vinegar is filtered into bottles through a muslin-lined funnel, corked and laid down. It improves with age.

Meanwhile, the *vinaigrier* is refilled to the level of the aeration hole with 14 bottles of red wine, themselves filled from leftover glasses and bottle ends, corked and stored in waiting. Vinegar is never drawn off nor wine added to the keg between filling and emptying.

Vinaigrette: I am not happy with a meal unless it contains something green but if that, perhaps idiosyncratic, requirement is fulfilled elsewhere on the menu, I rarely bother any more to serve a green salad between the main course and the cheese. My personal preference is, increasingly, to place any preparation in vinaigrette at the beginning of a meal, even if it be nothing more than a green, leafy salad. I have often noted that whereas guests devour opening salads with relish, they usually only serve themselves a couple of symbolic leaves of a salad after a main course and proceed to pick at them disinterestedly. There is no reason, however, why a green salad, sprinkled with herbs, could not be placed in its traditional slot on any of the menus in the following chapters.

For most purposes, the best vinaigrette contains nothing but salt, pepper, good vinegar and good olive oil. There is no reason, ever, to prepare vinaigrette in advance or to seal it into a bottle and shake it to death – vinaigrette is not and should not be an emulsion. Nor should it be refrigerated, which devitalises it. Tossed green salads are attractive only before they are tossed. The simplest presentation consists in mixing together the salt, pepper and vinegar in the bottom of the salad bowl, stirring in the olive oil, crossing the salad servers in the bowl and tumbling over a choice of green, leafy things with chopped herbs sprinkled atop. If tender, sweet lettuces are used, about one part of vinegar to four or five of oil is right and chopped *fines-herbes*, including tarragon, are a logical surface scattering; if spicy, bitter green things – rocket, dandelion, wild chicory, purslane, etc. – dominate, then one part of vinegar to three of oil will do and herbs such as hyssop, basil, tender spring savory and serpolet thyme will work better. Parsley and chives mingle well with everything.

Grilled peppers and grated carrots seem, in particular, to cry out for garlic in their vinaigrettes. To prepare a garlic vinaigrette, I pound a small clove of garlic with coarse salt and ground pepper in a mortar to a paste with no fragment of solid remnant before dissolving it in the vinegar (for peppers, their juices are then added) and stirring in the oil. Grated carrots should be stirred, turned and tossed thoroughly in the vinaigrette before being loosely spooned on to their serving dish; universally considered by self-styled gourmets to be detestably banal, they are wonderful when seasoned correctly and beautiful when presented with a feathery sprinkling of parsley threads. Chopped hard-boiled eggs and parsley can be stirred into a vinaigrette and spread over leeks, first cleaned, tied in a bundle like asparagus, parboiled until just tender, drained, sponged in a towel and laid out, still hot or tepid, on a platter.

Mustard, however good in a lemon and cream dressing, has no place in a vinaigrette unless it be to disguise bad vinegar and bad oil.

BASIC RECIPES
AND TECHNIQUES

MIREPOIX

INGREDIENTS
METRIC AND IMPERIAL

olive oil or butter

carrots, split, core removed if necessary, and chopped

onions, chopped

small celery stick, diced

large pinch of dried mixed herbs (page 14), to which a small pinch of pulverised bay leaf may be added, if desired

salt

Mirepoix is mainly used as an aromatic base for braised meats and vegetables; it can also be added to soups or stuffings, or be used, held in place by a caul wrapper, to coat flattened small birds, poultry breasts, rabbit fillets or cutlets for grilling; it can also be spread, beneath the skin, on the breast of a chicken to be roasted or grilled and so forth. The fineness to which the vegetables are chopped depends on the use to which the mirepoix is put and, for braised foods, on the length of cooking time: a finely chopped mirepoix will disintegrate in a long braising process; coarsely chopped, it will not release its ultimate flavour in a short process. In long braising, the mirepoix is usually strained out of the braising liquids and discarded; for shorter braising periods, if the mirepoix is to be retained, it is best to first pry free and discard any woody or yellowish cores from the split carrots before chopping them. To chop them coarsely, split the halves, gather together the quarters and slice them into short lengths; to chop them finely, slice the halves finely lengthwise, then slice into match-sticks; gather together the mass and slice finely crosswise, guiding the knife blade with the knuckles of in-turned fingertips.

In his quest for pure flavours and clean sauces, Alexandre Dumaine, during his 30-year reign in Saulieu, developed an alternative method to the following recipe which eliminates the fat. Spread the dry ingredients in the bottom of a heavy oven casserole and sweat them, covered, in a preheated 190°C (375°F or Mark 5) oven for 20–30 minutes with an occasional stir. Uncover and cook for 5–10 minutes longer with several stirs until their moisture evaporates, signs of golden caramelisation appear and the vegetables begin to stick to the bottom of the utensil, at which point it is removed from the oven and deglazed with a few drops of white wine while being scraped with a wooden spoon to dissolve the colour.

Here's a favourite starter, to be washed down with a simple white wine: trim artichokes, rub with lemon juice, and push into a bed of mirepoix in an earthenware *poêlon*, with no space to waste. Add a bouquet garni, a few grains of coriander, a handful of unpeeled, lightly crushed garlic cloves and salt. Sprinkle liberally with olive oil and white wine, press a sheet of oiled greaseproof paper to the surface, cover tightly and braise gently for 45 minutes (artichokes to be turned after 20 minutes) or until the artichokes are tender. Serve tepid or at room temperature.

For a mirepoix, use approximately equal quantities of carrots and onions. The weights and chopping styles are suggested in the recipes in which the mirepoix is used.

Put enough olive oil or melted butter in a heavy sauté pan, or the pan that is to be used for cooking, to film the bottom of the pan. Add the remaining ingredients and sweat together over very low heat for about 30 minutes, stirring occasionally, until yellowed and softened but not browned. The pan may be kept covered for the first 15 minutes or so of cooking.

LITTLE STOCKS

INGREDIENTS
METRIC AND IMPERIAL

1–2 carrots, each cut into 3–4 pieces

2 onions, quartered

2–3 garlic cloves, unpeeled, bruised

1 small celery stick, or sprig of fresh lovage

2–3 large sprigs of fresh thyme

1 bay leaf

1 parsley root, if available, scraped and washed, or parsley stalks

depending on the stock's use and what is at hand: poultry carcass, wingtips and neck, broken or cut up, or lean beef and veal trimmings (or 'stewing' meat), broken-up veal knuckle, etc.

salt

The stocks of the home kitchen are leftover *pot-au-feu* or *poule-au-pot* broths´ or little essences eked out of bones, broken-up carcasses, offal and trimmings of the principal ingredient of the dish in preparation, precious sources of flavour that are too often carelessly discarded. When stock is required for a braised vegetable, as for the artichoke bottoms in Chapter I, it can be made up from broken veal hock, beef and veal trimmings, chicken wingtips and necks, etc. Left-over, jellied roasting juices are valuable additions to any of these stocks (lamb juices are best re-served for lamb preparations). It is a mistake to imagine that stock cubes can replace home-made stock – they will only make your food taste dirty; pure water is a better substitute.

Choose a heavy saucepan large enough so that it will be no more than two-thirds filled when all the ingredients are arranged in it. Place the vegetables and herbs in the bottom (to prevent the meats from touching and sticking to the pan), then arrange the meats and/or poultry pieces on top so as to take up no more space than necessary. Salt lightly and pour over cold water to a level of at least 5 cm (2 in) above that of the solids. Bring slowly to the boiling point over low to mode-rate heat, removing and discard-ing the grey scum that rises to the surface. Adjust the heat (with the help of an asbestos plaque or other heat diffuser, if necessary) so that, covered with the lid slightly ajar, a bare simmer can be maintained. Leave to cook for at least 3–4 hours. During this time, the contents of the sauce-pan should never be stirred or displaced, lest the deposits on the sides and bottom cloud the stock; they should, however, always remain immersed and it may be necessary to pour over boiling water gently at some point during the cooking period.

Pour the contents of the sauce-pan into a large, fine-meshed sieve, or a colander lined with moistened and wrung-out mus-lin or cheesecloth, placed over a large bowl; remove the sieve or colander to another bowl to drain completely and join the drained stock to the other. When the fat rises to the surface, re-move as much as possible (or, if prepared in advance, leave the stock to cool, refrigerate it, un-covered, and lift off the fat after it solidifies).

For the recipes in this book, it may be preferable to concentrate the flavours of the stock by re-duction, which will permit you, at the same time, to remove any remaining traces of fat: choose a saucepan which will be filled close to the brim by the stock (to facilitate skimming). Bring it to the boil, then move the saucepan half off the heat and adjust the heat to maintain a light boil on the heated side of the stock's surface. As a skin forms on the quiet surface, pull it to the far edge, away from the heat, with the side of a tablespoon and re-move it. Repeat the skimming at unhurried intervals until no more fat appears in the forming skin. Move the saucepan back over the heat, turn it up some-what, and reduce to the desired concentration.

BASIC SAUSAGE MEAT

INGREDIENTS
METRIC AND IMPERIAL

900 g (2 lb) fresh pork without bones, such as belly, shoulder, blade, back fat

coarse salt

fine salt and freshly ground pepper (with allspice)

1 tsp mixed dried herbs (page 14)

3–4 tbsp white wine

Use approximately two parts lean pork to one part fat.

Liberally sprinkle the pieces of pork on all sides with coarse salt. Place in a non-metallic con-tainer, cover and leave to salt down overnight. Discard the li-quid that is given off, rinse the pieces well and dry them. Cut them up and pass them through the medium blade of a mincer, not a processor. Season abund-antly with pepper, and salt to taste (you may want to fry a teaspoonful and judge for salt before adding more – the overnight salting down serves mostly to draw out the liquids and will have salted the meats only slightly). Add the herbs and wine and mix very thoroughly, using your hands.

TO TURN ARTICHOKES

Avoid artichokes with dried, discoloured outer leaves. Size is not an indication of age. Whether they be globe artichokes or one of the more elongated varieties, the contour at the base of the leaves should describe a clean curve and the stem should be thick in relation to the size of the artichoke. Narrow, fibrous stems and an indented profile above the base of the artichoke are indications of age and toughness. Given these signs – and on condition that there is enough stem to grasp hold of (in France, artichokes are sold with their stems – this is not always true elsewhere) – the stem should be broken off, rather than cut, at the base, pulling out the fibrous strings which, otherwise, remain lodged in the bottom.

Cut surfaces of artichokes rapidly discolour when exposed to air unless rubbed with or dipped into lemon juice; carbon steel knives blacken the flesh on contact. Keep a bowl containing a bit of lemon juice at hand while working and use a sharp, stainless steel paring knife.

To turn an artichoke, first break or cut off the stem at the base and remove the dozen or so tough, outer leaves, bending each backward until the tender flesh at the base of the inner surface snaps before pulling downward to remove the tough leaf, its tender base remaining attached to the artichoke bottom. Slice off the top half or two-thirds of the artichoke, depending on where the inner leaves turn tender. Holding the artichoke upside-down, begin

turning at the stem end, keeping the knife more or less stationary while turning the artichoke in a spiralling fashion and removing all of the dark green surface to expose the pale green flesh. Dip or rub regularly with lemon as you work. Turn the artichoke over and trim the extremities of the outer leaves; the shape of the turned artichoke will approximate a flattened sphere.

Both recipes using artichokes in this book call for raw artichoke bottoms (when a preparation calls for precooked artichoke bottoms, the chokes are not removed until after cooking). For bottoms to be used whole, the chokes must be pried out with a teaspoon, the inside bottom scraped clean with the spoon and immediately doused with lemon. If they are to be sliced, it is easier to halve the bottoms first and to cut out the chokes carefully with a knife-tip.

TO PEEL (OR BLANCH) ALMONDS AND PISTACHIOS

Plunge shelled almonds or pistachios into boiling water, return to the boil, leave for a few seconds, then drain and rub them briskly in a folded towel or between two towels; most will be freed of their skins and the remainder will slip out easily if pinched. In a batch of pistachios, some are always yellow; it is best to discard these, both for flavour and appearance.

PASTRY

INGREDIENTS
METRIC AND IMPERIAL

150 g (5 oz) plain flour
salt
150 g (5 oz) cold butter, diced
4–6 tbsp cold water

For my purposes, I have settled on a single method for making both short and puff pastry, using approximately equal weights of flour and butter. If you prefer to use less butter for short pastry, it can be reduced to as little as half the weight of the flour with good results; to be transformed into puff pastry, best results can be had only with the maximum measure of butter.

Sift the flour and salt into a large mixing bowl. Add the butter and, with two table-knives, blades crossed and touching, cut through the flour and butter, pulling the knives apart rapidly and repeatedly until the flour is slightly mealy and the cubes of butter are slightly and irregularly reduced in size. Add only enough water, stirring and pressing with a fork, to pull the contents of the bowl into a coherent mass that can be gathered together into a compact ball in your hands. Wrap and chill for 20–30 minutes in a freezer, or for an hour in a refrigerator.

For short pastry: dust the work surface lightly with flour, place the ball of dough on it and flatten it slightly with the palm of your hand. Dust its surface lightly with flour, give it a few light blows with the rolling pin, then roll it out partially. Fold it twice (any way), reform it to a flat, round shape with your hands, and dust the dough and the work surface again with flour if necessary. Roll it out to a circle somewhat larger than the mould, roll it loosely around the rolling pin, brushing off any free flour; and unroll it over the mould. Press it into place.

Trim the edges, leaving a slight overhang – any short edges can be patched with fragments of trimming, their edges first moistened before being pressed into place. Roll the outer edge under, press it to the border of the mould all the way round, and crimp it with the side of your thumb, dipped repeatedly in flour. Prick the bottom and the sides of the pastry case with a fork. Chill in the refrigerator or freezer long enough to firm up the pastry. One should work rapidly and handle the pastry as little as possible while getting it together. If, before finally rolling it out, it becomes soft and sticky, firm it up in the refrigerator or the freezer before continuing.

To blind bake, press a sheet of greaseproof paper into place in the pastry-lined mould and fill with dried beans, rice or specially designed metal pellets. Place the mould in a preheated 200°C (400°F or Mark 6) oven, reduce the thermostat to 180°C (350°F or Mark 4) and bake for 15 minutes. Remove the paper and its filling and return the pastry shell to the oven to bake for 5 minutes longer to dry it out.

For puff pastry: flatten the dough and beat it lightly as for short pastry. Roll it out into an elongated band, fold the two ends in to meet each other and fold again in the middle to make four layers. Give the folded pastry a quarter of a turn so that the folded edges face you, then roll it out again to a band and fold as before. Wrap and chill in the freezer until hard but not frozen. Return to the work surface, beat lightly to make the dough more supple, then roll out and fold twice, as before, with a quarter of a turn each time between rolling out and folding. Repeat this once again after a rest in the freezer, or, if you like, roll it out and fold it only once the following time, then roll it out for using.

SABAYON SAUCE

INGREDIENTS
METRIC AND IMPERIAL

2 egg yolks

1 heaped tbsp caster sugar

4 tbsp white wine

Serves 4

Sabayon sauce is most interesting when a fine wine with very pronounced aromas is used in its confection; those which have given me the greatest pleasure are old Sauternes and Alsatian Gewürztraminer. The sauce is very rich in effect; this recipe may seem like very little but it will adequately serve 4 – or it may be doubled. Remember that the sauce will double in volume so choose your saucepan accordingly. Prepare the *bain-marie* first, placing a trivet in the bottom of a larger saucepan and pouring in enough water to immerse by one-third to one-half the smaller saucepan as it rests on the trivet.

In a small saucepan, whisk together the egg yolks and sugar until lightened in colour. Add the wine and immerse in the *bain-marie*, in hot but not boiling water, over low heat. Whisk until the sauce is thickened and its volume doubled. Lower the heat if the water threatens to boil, removing the saucepan momentarily while continuing to whisk – or raise the heat if the process is taking too long. Remove from the heat and continue whisking until the saucepan has had time to lose the heat absorbed from the hot water.

RASPBERRY SAUCE

INGREDIENTS
METRIC AND IMPERIAL

225 g (8 oz) fresh or frozen raspberries

caster sugar

Serves 4

Pass the raspberries through a nylon or stainless steel sieve with a wooden pestle. Stir in sugar to taste.

KEY TO MAP

1
1 CHABLIS GRAND CRU
2 CHABLIS; PETIT CHABLIS
3 GEVREY-CHAMBERTIN
4 MOREY-SAINT-DENIS
5 CHAMBOLLE-MUSIGNY
6 VOUGEOT
7 VOSNE-ROMANEE
8 NUITS-SAINT-GEORGES
9 ALOXE-CORTON
10 BEAUNE
11 POMMARD
12 VOLNAY
13 MEURSAULT
14 PULIGNY-MONTRACHET
15 CHASSAGNE-MONTRACHET
16 SANTENAY
17 RULLY; MERCUREY
18 GIVRY
19 MONTAGNY

2
1 MACONNAIS
2 POUILLY-FUISSE
3 BEAUJOLAIS
4 SAINT-AMOUR
5 JULIENAS; CHENAS
6 MOULIN-A-VENT
7 FLEURIE
8 CHIROUBLES
9 MORGON
10 BROUILLY; COTE DE BROUILLY

3
1 COTE ROTIE
2 CONDRIEU
3 SAINT-JOSEPH
4 HERMITAGE
5 CROZES-HERMITAGE
6 CORNAS
7 SAINT-PERAY

4
1 LIRAC
2 TAVEL
3 BEAUMES-DE-VENISE
4 CHATEAUNEUF-DU-PAPE
5 PALETTE
6 CASSIS
7 BANDOL
8 BELLET

5
1 JURANCON
2 MADIRAN
3 COTES DE BUZET
4 COTE DE MARMANDAIS
5 COTES DE DURAS
6 MONBAZILLAC
7 CAHORS
8 BERGERAC
9 MINERVOIS
10 CORBIERES
11 COLLIOURE
12 BANYULS

6
1 PESSAC
2 LEOGNAN
3 GRAVES
4 SAUTERNES

7
1 MEDOC
2 SAINT-ESTEPHE
3 PAUILLAC
4 SAINT-JULIEN
5 LISTRAC
6 MOULIS
7 MARGAUX
8 HAUT-MEDOC
9 POMEROL
10 SAINT-EMILION

8
1 MUSCADET
2 MUSCADET DE SEVRE-ET-MAINE
3 MUSCADET DES COTEAUX DE LA LOIRE
4 SAVENNIERES
5 QUARTS-DE-CHAUME
6 COTEAUX DU LAYON
7 BONNEZEAUX
8 SAUMUR-CHAMPIGNY
9 SAINT-NICOLAS-DE-BOURGEUIL
10 BOURGEUIL
11 CHINON
12 VOUVRAY
13 SANCERRE
14 POUILLY-SUR-LOIRE; POUILLY FUME

9
1 ARBOIS
2 PUPILLIN
3 CHATEAU-CHALON
4 ETOILE

10
1 RIBEAUVILLE
2 RIQUEWIHR
3 KAYERSBERG
4 WINTZENHEIM
5 EGUISHEIM

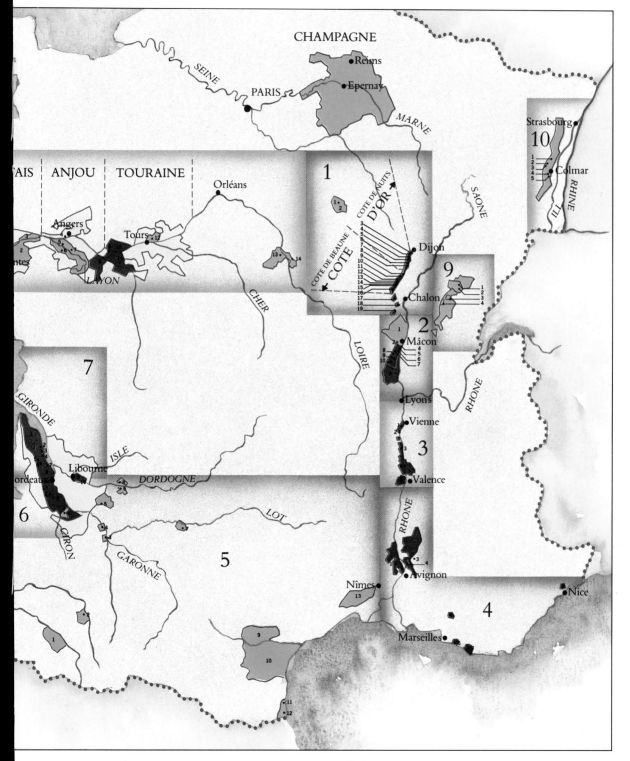

CHAMPAGNE

Reims

Epernay

PARIS

SEINE

MARNE

Strasbourg

10

Colmar

RHINE

ILL

ANJOU TOURAINE

Orléans

1

CÔTE DE NUITS

CÔTE D'OR

SAÔNE

Angers

Tours

CÔTE DE BEAUNE

CÔTE

Dijon

9

LAYON

CHER

Chalon

LOIRE

2

Mâcon

7

Lyons

Vienne

RHÔNE

ISLE

DORDOGNE

GIRONDE

Libourne

3

Valence

Bordeaux

GIRON

LOT

GARONNE

5

RHÔNE

6

Nîmes

Avignon

Nice

4

Marseilles

Northern Burgundy

The most sublime wines of Burgundy come from the Côte d'Or, a strip of vineyards some 30 miles long and a mile, more or less, wide. The *côte* is the hillside on which they are planted; *or* is an abbreviation of orient; thus, la Côte d'Or means the hillside with an eastern exposure. The northern half is the Côte de Nuits, which produces Burgundy's greatest red wines; the southern half is the Côte de Beaune, which produces fine red wines and Burgundy's greatest whites. Journalists who have adopted the wine writer's standard vocabulary find the red wines reminiscent of cherries, raspberries, strawberries, liquorice, truffles, violets, velvet and silk; the whites of hazelnuts, almonds, grilled bread, honey, peaches, hawthorn, locust and so forth.

Delicacy, subtlety and nuance are the hallmark of fine Burgundies. They are also fragile wines and the reds, in particular, are perhaps the most susceptible of all wines to travel damage and mistreatment. Except for certain generic appellations, the reds are made from the Pinot noir grape and the whites from Chardonnay (very small quantities of Nuits-Saint-Georges la Perrière and Morey-Saint-Denis Monts-Luisants, in the Côte de Nuits, are made from the Pinot blanc grape; in the Côte Chalonnaise, Pinot blanc sometimes complements the Chardonnay).

Today's official classification of the wines of the Côte d'Or varies only in minor detail from attempts at classification two centuries ago. The rare and expensive great growths (Grands Crus) carry only the name of the vineyard, with no reference to village origin, on the label. In a publication dated 1752, one reads, 'Le Montrachet and la Romanée are two extremely limited growths. These two wines, for this reason, are the first and the

Apéritif: Aligoté de Bouzeron or a white Côte Chalonnaise
(Rully or Montagny)

Scrambled Eggs with Asparagus
CHABLIS PREMIER CRU MONTEE
DE TONNERRE 1984
(or a white Côte de Beaune: Auxey-Duresses,
Pernand-Vergelesses, Meursault, etc.)

Roast Beef, Braised Artichoke Bottoms with Glazed
Onions
VOLNAY CHAMPANS 1982
(or another red Côte de Beaune: Chassagne-Montrachet,
Santenay, Pommard, Beaune, etc.)

Cheeses
LATRICIERES-CHAMBERTIN 1981
(or another Côte de Nuits: a first growth or Premier Cru
from Nuits-Saint-Georges, Vosne-Romanée, Chambolle-
Musigny, Morey-Saint-Denis or Gevrey-Chambertin or a
Grand Cru: Musigny, Richebourg, La Tâche, Grands-
Echézeaux, etc.)

Honey Ice Cream, Raspberry Sauce

most sought after in all of Burgundy.' This was written eight years before the Prince de Conti purchased la Romanée and added his name to it; the wine that is called 'la Romanée' today was assembled in the nineteenth century from a number of fragments of Richebourg and so-baptised to capitalise on the name of its famous neighbour. The observation is as true today as it was during the reign of Louis XV.

Down a rung from the summit, the first growths (Premiers Crus) must mention the village or the name of the vineyard, or both, followed by the words Premier Cru; further down the ladder, the simple village appellations carry only the name of the village or, if the place name is mentioned, it must be in smaller letters; beyond these are the generic appellations.

There is one area of difficulty in all this. At different times during the nineteenth century, legislation was passed permitting each of the villages of Gevrey, Chambolle, Vosne, Nuits, Aloxe, Puligny and Chassagne to add the name of its greatest growth to its own (respectively -Chambertin, -Musigny, -Romanée, -Saint-Georges, -Corton and, for Puligny and Chassagne, whose boundaries are straddled by le Montrachet, -Montrachet). These measures were no doubt commercially astute and must have been applauded by growers who owned no great growths, but they have led to a deplorable confusion in the minds of many who are unable to distinguish between a village appellation and a great growth.

My personal loyalty to Burgundy has never wavered since my first bottle of La Tâche (a transcendent 1951, considered to be one of the worst vintages of the century), drunk in 1954, at Alexandre Dumaine's Hôtel de la Côte d'Or in Saulieu, with a truffled chicken steamed in the vapours of a concentrated stock. Last tasted a year ago, it is still a lovely wine, now fragile and lacy. It was the memory of another Tâche, a 1954 shared with Aubert de Villaine, co-proprietor of the Domaine de la Romanée Conti, over roast beef a couple of years ago, which determined me to place roast beef on this menu. (For the cheeses that evening, I had already opened a Mouton-Rothschild 1962, under any other circumstances a beautiful wine; it was absolutely crushed by the ethereal presence of La Tâche.)

Both the red and the white wines from the Côte Chalonnaise are similar to the village appellations of the

Côte de Beaune, often at more interesting prices.

Eggs, asparagus and artichokes are all said by the lawmakers to be incompatible with wine. You will have to judge for yourself. To me, eggs are a perfect vehicle for other flavours, asparagus and truffles being my two favourite garnishes to scrambled eggs. I have served asparagus often with a Chablis Premier Cru Montée de Tonnerre 1984 and been ravished by the marriage. Chablis, halfway between the Côte d'Or and Champagne, produces white wines, steely and flinty in youth, which, when made with grapes from old vines, traditionally vinified and raised in oak, age well, deepening in colour from pale green-gold to burnished gold, rounding out and revealing unexpected depths. It is true that artichokes impose their own flavour on wine – rather pleasantly, in fact, but often masking the wine's native qualities – when they are unaltered by braising and the absorption of other flavours. I do not think that happens with the recipe given in this chapter.

Most traditional Burgundian dishes, densely flavoured like the various red wine stews – coq-au-vin, boeuf à la bourguignonne, matelote of eel – or violently flavoured like jambon persillé or escargots à la bourguignonne, seem to me, wonderful though they are, to be more at home with something less grand than Burgundy's finest wines. I would willingly place a red Mercurey, from the Côte Chalonnaise, on a coq-au-vin and the pleasant and refreshing Bourgogne Aligoté, made from the aligoté grape, on garlicky snails, but delicate wines really demand gentle and uncomplicated flavours. With the reds, you can't beat a plain roast. I have chosen Roast Beef for sentimental reasons but lamb, poultry or game birds will also serve. In order to be able to present more than one red Burgundy on this menu, I have nonetheless placed the great growth on the cheeses, and one should take care that they not be violent.

TIMING

The artichokes and onions may be prepared in advance and rewarmed, the sauce reduced and finished at the last minute. The croûtons and the asparagus should be prepared before the roast is put to cook. For a roast that requires approximately half an hour (the resting period is elastic), put it into the oven just before putting the eggs to cook.

SCRAMBLED EGGS WITH ASPARAGUS

INGREDIENTS
METRIC AND IMPERIAL

450 g (1 lb) asparagus

salt and freshly ground pepper

100 g (4 oz) cold unsalted butter, diced

10–12 eggs

1 garlic clove

FOR THE CROUTONS

2–3 slices of day-old firm-textured bread, crust removed

about 15 g (½ oz) unsalted butter

Serves 4

The most important quality of scrambled eggs, as I understand them, is that they be of a smooth, voluptuous, creamy, thickly pourable consistency, without lumps or curds. To achieve this, they are cooked in a *bain-marie*, a large saucepan with a trivet placed in the bottom upon which to rest a smaller saucepan, the larger pan filled with enough hot water to immerse the smaller pan partially.

I have more than once read that perfect scrambled eggs can only be prepared in small quantities. This is nonsense. I find scrambled eggs with asparagus, something which requires little concentration when one is subjected to a milling crowd and multiple conversations, to be one of the most practical and most appreciated of starters. One must not be impatient – it may take half to three-quarters of an hour for a large number of eggs (say 35–40 for 12 servings) to arrive at the proper consistency – and the water must not be permitted to reach the boil. It is, in fact, easier to produce perfect scrambled eggs in large quantities than in small.

Carefully peel the asparagus to remove all tough or stringy parts of the stalks, then slice the spears thinly on the bias, leaving the tips intact. Set aside.

Before beginning to cook the eggs, prepare the croûtons. Cut the bread into small cubes. In a frying pan, over low heat, cook the cubes of bread in the butter, tossing regularly and adding more butter as needed, until the cubes of bread are golden and crisp without being completely dried out. Place the frying pan in a warm corner.

Plunge the sliced asparagus into heavily salted, boiling water and return to a full, rolling boil, then pour into a sieve to drain and hold in waiting.

Add salt, pepper and about 25 g (1 oz) of the chopped butter to the eggs and break them up with a fork, whisking only enough to mix them. Pour into a buttered saucepan and place in the *bain-marie*. Rub the garlic over a wooden spoon and use this to stir the eggs, slowly and regularly, back and forth and around, scraping sides, corners and bottom all the while. Turn the heat up or down as necessary but do not let the water approach a boil. As the eggs begin to thicken, watch them closely, stirring more rapidly. Remove the pan from the hot water, continuing to stir as they approach the desired consistency. Add most of the remaining chopped butter, stirring until it is absorbed into the eggs.

In an omelette pan, toss the asparagus in the remaining butter over high heat for a few seconds to reheat it, then stir into the eggs. Serve on warm but not hot plates, with croûtons scattered over.

NOTE

Buttering the saucepan only partially prevents the eggs from sticking; they will still leave a film of cooked egg on the sides and bottom of the pan. When removed from the hot water, the eggs continue thickening from the heat retained by the saucepan; heavy copper retains heat longer than other materials and should be removed from the *bain-marie* at an earlier stage. It is better to remove the eggs too early and to return them for a moment to the hot water, if necessary, than to risk having overcooked eggs; they should not, however, be returned to the hot water after the remaining butter has been added. If the plates are hotter than the eggs themselves, the eggs will overcook on contact.

Scrambled Eggs with Asparagus served with Chablis

ROAST BEEF

If possible, find a butcher who knows his business and trade with him regularly; the best cuts always go to the regular customers who know what they want. Beef need not be aged for months, but a side of beef that has hung in the cold room for a week or 10 days before being cut up gains both in tenderness and in flavour.

The characteristic clean, robust flavour of beef is not improved by the association with herbs or marinades. It is important that the roast be at room temperature when put to cook; remove it from the refrigerator an hour or two in advance, depending on its size. Depending also on its size, a roast should rest in a warm place for 15 to 45 minutes after the initial cooking, during which time the heat, superficially absorbed from a hot oven, penetrates to the heart of the roast, the interior temperature continuing to rise, and the juices are re-integrated into the flesh, which at the same time becomes more tender, losing a certain rubbery resiliency. If nothing else is being cooked in the oven, it is the obvious resting place; remove the meat from the oven for a few minutes to stop the cooking, leave the oven door open until the oven cools slightly and return the meat to the closed oven.

The way in which a roast of beef is cooked depends on its size, its shape and the tenderness of the cut. Tender meat cooks more rapidly than a firm cut (and aged meat more rapidly than fresh) and the thickness of the cut is a more important factor in determining the cooking time than the actual weight – a 1.4 kg (3 lb) section of contre-filet will require hardly less cooking time than one twice its weight, that is to say, of the same thickness but of twice the length.

Firm cuts such as chuck or shoulder roasts (the cut known in England as 'leg of mutton') or back rib (neck end) are best cooked long and slowly without an initial searing. For a 3 kg (6½ lb) roast, count about 25 minutes per 450 g (1 lb) at 140°C (275°F or Mark 1).

For a whole fillet or tenderloin, first trim it, removing all fat and surface membranes, fold back the slender tip, or filet-mignon, and tie it to equalise the roast's thickness. Rub all over with softened butter or olive oil, season and put into the oven preheated to 260°C (500°F or Mark 10). Cook for 8 to 10 minutes, or until sizzling, then turn off the oven and forget it for 20 to 30 minutes. (If you imagine that you do not like very rare beef, don't waste your money on tenderloin; overcooked, it is dry, tasteless and, at best, boring food – you will be better served by a slow-roasted shoulder cut at a much lower price.)

Following a couple of other indications, which may be subject to alteration in terms of intuition or personal taste: Contre-filet or top-loin, often called, in England, entrecôte: 4 to 7 minutes per 450 g (1 lb); 230°C (450°F or Mark 8) for the first 10 minutes, the remainder at 160°C (325°F or Mark 3) plus a 15 minute rest. Rib roast (the first three ribs after the floating ribs for best results; ask the butcher to chine it for easy carving):

8 to 10 minutes per 450 g (1 lb); 230°C (450° or Mark 8) for the first 10 minutes with progressive reduction, first to 180°C (350°F to Mark 4), then 150°C (300°F or Mark 2) plus a 30 to 45 minute rest.

BRAISED ARTICHOKE BOTTOMS
WITH GLAZED ONIONS

It is not convenient to give specific measures for stock and wine here; the quantity depends on the shape of the cooking vessel and how closely the artichoke bottoms fit into it. It should be of a non-reactive material, preferably earthenware or, lacking that, enamelled ironware or heavy stainless steel.

Arrange the artichoke bottoms in the cooking vessel. Pour stock and wine into and around to half immerse them (two parts stock to one of wine) and bring to the boil. Cook, covered, at a bare simmer for about 40 minutes, or until the artichoke bottoms are tender but still slightly resistant to the prick of a trussing needle, turning them over in their cooking liquid after 20 minutes. Remove the bottoms to a plate; pour the liquid into a small saucepan, return the bottoms to their casserole and hold them, covered, while reducing the cooking liquid by half. Pour the liquid back over the bottoms, spoon over the cream and cook again, covered, at a gentle simmer for another 15 to 20 minutes, basting occasionally.

Meanwhile, put the peeled onions into a saucepan of a size that will just hold them in a single layer. Add the butter, sugar, salt and enough water to immerse them only partially. Bring the water to the boil and cook, covered, for 8 to 10 minutes, until the onions are barely tender, shaking the pan gently from time to time. Uncover them and cook, shaking regularly, over higher heat until no liquid is left and the onions are uncoloured but glossy. (If preparing them ahead of time, do not completely reduce the liquid; it will finish reducing with the reheating.)

Place the artichoke bottoms on a warmed serving dish, spoon the onions into their cavities and pour the sauce through a small sieve held over the artichoke bottoms.

INGREDIENTS
METRIC AND IMPERIAL

1 or 2 raw artichoke bottoms (page 20) per person, depending on size

stock (page 18)

fortified wine such as port, Madeira or sherry (I used old sherry)

4–5 tbsp double cream

FOR THE ONIONS

20–30 small pickling onions

10 g (⅓ oz) unsalted butter

small pinch of sugar

salt

Serves 4

Overleaf: (top to bottom) Tommette de Savoie, Pont L'Evêque, four goat cheeses, Epoisses, and Cantal with a Burgundy Grand Cru from the village of Gevrey-Chambertin.

HONEY ICE CREAM

I use lavender honey made by bees which have fed on flowers from the lavender fields of the Alpine foothills. In autumn, when it is fresh, it is thick but liquid; as the year progresses, it solidifies. Use liquid honey, if possible. If your honey has crystallised, scoop it into a bowl and immerse it in hot water for a few minutes before trying to incorporate the other ingredients.

Bring the milk to the boil. Whisk together the eggs, honey and salt and slowly pour in the milk, whisking the while. Stir in the cream with the whisk and leave to cool. Pour the cooled mixture through a strainer into another bowl and then into the ice cream maker, following instructions that accompany your maker.

Serve with a sauceboat of Raspberry Sauce on the side.

Honey Ice Cream with Raspberry Sauce

INGREDIENTS
METRIC AND IMPERIAL

500 ml (16 fl oz) milk

5 eggs

2 heaped tbsp honey, or to taste

small pinch of salt

250 ml (8 fl oz) double cream

TO SERVE
Raspberry Sauce (page 21)

Serves 4

Southern Burgundy

For all practical purposes, it is easiest to think of Mâconnais wines as white and Beaujolais as red. Red wine production in the Mâconnais has been on the decline for some time and much of the red wine still made there is labelled generically with no indication of regional origin. The best of what was once Beaujolais blanc now bears the Saint-Véran appellation.

The white wines of the Mâconnais are made from Chardonnay, sometimes in combination with Pinot blanc. Pouilly-Fuissé is the most celebrated and by far the most expensive; one of the best is Château Fuissé. It is a common complaint in Britain that the American taste for Pouilly-Fuissé has sent the prices soaring. At their best, the neighbouring Pouilly-Vinzelles and Pouilly-Loché are similar in style and more affordable. Mâcon-Villages or the other Mâcon whites which take the name of a specific village – Mâcon-Viré, Mâcon-Lugny, etc. – are pleasant and refreshing, good as apéritif and hors d'oeuvre wines. They do not have the dimension of the white Burgundies from the Côte de Beaune, but the price is attractive and they are easy to drink.

Red Beaujolais is made from the Gamay grape (Gamay *à jus blanc* – white-juiced Gamay) which finds its natural ally in the granitic soils of the local hillsides. It is, by nature, an abundant producer.

The classification hierarchy in Beaujolais begins with the simple appellations, Beaujolais and Beaujolais Supérieur, produced in the southern part of the region, not far from Lyons. They are followed first by Beaujolais-Villages, which may come from any of some 30 communities, then by the nine first-growth village appellations: Brouilly, Côte de Brouilly, Morgon, Chiroubles, Fleurie, Moulin-à-Vent, Chénas, Juliénas and

Apéritif: Mâcon-Villages

Stuffed Onions Baked in Cream Sauce
MACON-VILLAGES
(or Pouilly-Fuissé, Pouilly-Loché, Pouilly-Vinzelles,
Saint-Vérand, Macon-Viré, etc.)

Truffled Sausage with Pistachios in Court-bouillon,
New Potatoes in their Skins
MACON-VILLAGES
(or Beaujolais-Villages)

Pig's Trotters and Cabbage Braised in Beaujolais
COTE DE BROUILLY
(or Morgon, Chiroubles or Juliénas)

Cheeses
FLEURIE
(or Saint-Amour, Chénas or Moulin-à-Vent)

Macédoine of Fruits in Beaujolais

Saint-Amour, reading from south to north.

Today, Beaujolais is a sentimental memory. During the late fifties and early sixties, I bought and bottled, every month of April, a half keg (150 bottles) each of Beaujolais-Villages and Côte de Brouilly. They were my daily red table wines. Since then commercial success, the promotion machine and unrestrained production, coupled with modern oeno-technological methods of instant stabilisation, have flooded the world market with an industrialised, anonymous beverage.

It is a long time since I have drunk a cherry-coloured Beaujolais with the violet blush and the rush of green fruit which ravished me 30 years ago. It was a thing to be drunk young and cool, in abundance and joy, without too much thought, the perfect partner to the kind of *canaille* (riff-raffish) cuisine which one associates with Lyons. I would like to believe that there are still small growers who make Beaujolais as they, or their fathers, once did and who deliver it in casks to uncelebrated Lyonnais bistros to wash down charcuterie, ears, tails, testicles, tripe, trotters and whatnot; the bistros that I have tried in recent years all carry the heavily chaptalised Beaujolais of well-known *négociants* (chaptalisation being the addition of sugar to unfermented or partially fermented musts to raise the alcohol content of a wine).

Chaptalisation owes its name to Jean-Antoine Chaptal, Napoleon's Minister of the Interior, who recommended the judicious addition of sugar to grape musts as a corrective measure in deficient vintages; a Beaujolais *négociant* recently explained to me that, even in years when the grapes provide enough natural sugar to reach a normal balance of alcohol, the nature of Beaujolais imposes chaptalisation to give it the required velvety texture! In the past, no one expected to find velvet in a Beaujolais.

It is not easy, except for comparative tasting purposes, to create a suite of Beaujolais that makes any sense. In the following menu, it was my original intention (now disguised as alternative suggestions) to present the Mâcon-Villages as apéritif, followed by Pouilly-Fuissé, Beaujolais-Villages, one of the village growths and a Moulin-à-Vent. During the photography session, the realisation came too late that I had no Beaujolais-Villages in the cellar to photograph with the poached sausage and, in a moment of madness, I uncorked a Mâcon-Villages. Not that the marriage itself was unfortunate; the sausage takes equally well to a white wine as to a red. But that unreasoning gesture disrupted my plans for the sequence since it would be nonsense to precede a Mâcon-Villages by a Pouilly-Fuissé, and the appellations inferior to Mâcon-Villages, Mâcon Supérieur and Pinot-Chardonnay-Mâcon, are hardly ever seen for they are more easily commercialised under the generic label of Bourgogne blanc.

Moulin-à-Vent has pretensions to nobility and it is sometimes claimed that, after two or three years of bottle age, it resembles a Côte d'Or. The other wines, in any case, are all best drunk young, preferably before the following vintage, and well cooled. The quality of the fruit and the structure of the wine is so similar – and at the same time so uneven – from one village appellation to another that, whenever in a restaurant specialising in Beaujolais, I always ask the waiter or wine steward which is the lightest-bodied with the freshest fruit: I get a different answer every time, always take the advice given and am rarely satisfied.

TIMING

Nothing on this menu demands great precision. The onions may be stuffed, arranged in their gratin dish, protected by plastic film and refrigerated hours in advance if this is more convenient. The sausage will have been prepared several days or a week in advance and its court-bouillon may be prepared ahead of time; if the sausage is poached at the same time that the onions are baking, it may be held in its court-bouillon and, if necessary, gently rewarmed at the time of serving. Only the potatoes will suffer from being held and, depending on their size, should be put to cook when the onions are served. If preferred, the trotters may be half-braised the preceding day and put back to braise with the cabbage on the day of the meal; the dish will not suffer if braised half an hour longer than specified or if held for half an hour off the heat. The macedoine takes no time to prepare, an hour or so before going to table.

STUFFED ONIONS BAKED IN CREAM SAUCE

INGREDIENTS
METRIC AND IMPERIAL

3 or 4 very large sweet onions, weighing about 1.2 kg (2½ lb) in total

FOR THE STUFFING

450 g (1 lb) fresh spinach, trimmed

275 g (10 oz) ricotta or well-drained curd cheese

2 eggs

50 g (2 oz) Parmesan cheese, freshly grated

crumbled flowers of dried oregano

salt and freshly ground pepper

FOR THE SAUCE

250 ml (8 fl oz) double cream

150–175 ml (5–6 fl oz) fresh tomato purée (see below)

cayenne pepper

salt

Serves 4

The tomato purée, used in the sauce, is best prepared in summer from garden-ripe tomatoes. Coarsely chop them, then crush in a saucepan with a chopped onion, crushed garlic clove, a pinch of herbs and salt. Boil for 10 or 15 minutes and pass through a sieve. The heavy purée will rapidly settle to the bottom of the bowl, leaving a topaz-tinted liquid on the surface which can be ladled off (but not discarded; chilled, it is a delicious summer drink). The remaining purée may still have to be reduced a bit to gain body, but the less it has to cook the cleaner the flavour. Out of season, use canned tomatoes, drained of their liquid and puréed. Your own tomatoes, put up in glass jars, are the only ones which will taste of summer; next best are canned Italian plum tomatoes.

The onions are separated into concentric sheaths into which the stuffing is wrapped. The larger the onions, the more practical they are for this purpose. Make an incision, slicing with the grain or fibre (from top to bottom) to the heart of, or halfway into, each onion. Plunge them into a large pot of boiling water and cook, at a light boil, for 20 to 25 minutes, or until just supple enough for the layers to be separated. As they cook, they will open up, giving the appearance of a wedge having been cut out of each onion; using the tip of a trussing needle, test the heart of these openings to judge the moment they must be removed from the boiling water to a basin of cold water, to stop the cooking and to cool them for handling. Separate the successive layers, prying gently with fingertips, and lay them out on a towel to drain while preparing the stuffing. The outermost skin or layer will be overcooked and probably unusable; the hearts will be added to the stuffing.

Parboil the spinach leaves in a large pan of water for a few seconds, then drain and refresh under cold running water. Squeeze the spinach into a firm ball to expel excess liquid, then chop it. Chop the hearts of the parboiled onions.

Mash together the ricotta and eggs until smooth, add all the other stuffing ingredients and mix thoroughly. Taste for seasoning.

Lightly butter a large gratin dish. Place a tablespoonful of stuffing on each onion section and roll it up (some of the outer sections may be cut to serve for two rolls). Don't overstuff. Arrange the stuffed sections, seam side down, touching, in the gratin dish.

Preheat the oven to 180°C (350°F or Mark 4).

Whisk together the cream and tomato purée, season to taste with salt and cayenne and ladle over enough to coat the stuffed onions. Bake for about 45 minutes, spooning over more sauce if the onions show signs of drying up.

Stuffed Onions Baked in Cream Sauce

TRUFFLED SAUSAGE WITH PISTACHIOS
IN COURT-BOUILLON

INGREDIENTS
METRIC AND IMPERIAL

FOR THE SAUSAGE

about 2 m (2 yd) large sausage casing (pork or ox large intestine)

dash of vinegar

700 g (1½ lb) basic sausage meat (page 19)

225 g (8 oz) pork fillet, cut into ½–1 cm (¼–½ in) cubes

90 g (3½ oz) fresh pork back fat, diced

1 garlic clove, pounded to a paste with a pinch of coarse salt

about 40 g (1½ oz) shelled pistachios, peeled (page 20) and coarsely chopped

25–50 g (1–2 oz), or more, black truffle, diced

mixed dried herbs

about 4 tbsp Cognac

salt and freshly ground pepper

FOR THE COURT-BOUILLON

1 or 2 carrots, thinly sliced

1 medium onion, thinly sliced

parsley root or stalks

bay leaf, thyme and small sprig of lovage or small celery stalk

salt

white wine

Serves 4

Large intestine casings will make sausages approximately 5 cm (2 in) in diameter. To serve four as a first course, a sausage of about 20 cm (8 in) in length is right. It is impractical to make only one or two sausages and useful to make them of different lengths. Once made, they improve greatly if ripened for a few days or a week refrigerated with air circulating on all sides: place a wire rack or pastry grill, covered with a tea towel, on a tray, arrange the sausages, not touching, on top, cover loosely with another towel and refrigerate – or, if space permits, place directly on the refrigerator grill between two towels. Although not especially to be recommended, if, after a week's ripening, you have a surfeit of sausages, it is possible to freeze them, first wrapped air-tight in plastic film, then in foil.

Some of the ingredients for the sausage here are repetitions of those in basic sausage meat; use them accordingly, in consideration of the additional, unseasoned meats that have been added.

First soak the sausage casing in tepid water with a dash of vinegar for about 30 minutes. Drain and rinse well with cold running water from the tap, inside the casing as well, then press in towels to dry.

Mix together all of the ingredients for the sausage, using your hands, until thoroughly homogeneous.

A large plastic bottle, in which mineral waters or soft drinks are sold, cut off at the shoulder to form a funnel, is the perfect instrument for stuffing sausages. The sausage casing is pulled up on to the neck and held in place (released progressively when more length is needed) between forefinger and middle finger to either side of the neck, the thumb holding the funnel at the rim while, with the thumb of the other hand, the sausage mixture is forced into the casing. When the desired amount of mixture has gone in, tie the far end of the casing, first being careful to force out any air and leaving enough length at the end so that the tip of the casing may be folded over the knot and tied again. Mould the sausage with your hands, forcing out all air – no air pockets must remain – and giving it a slightly flattened form to ensure it is not overstuffed. Tie the other end in the same way.

Ripen the sausage for at least 3 or 4 days before using.

Prepare the court-bouillon long enough ahead of time so that it can cool down before the sausage is added. Choose an oval cocotte or a small fish kettle to economise on court-bouillon elements; the quantity of court-bouillon depends on the amount of liquid necessary to immerse the sausage in its chosen vessel.

Combine all the ingredients except the white wine, add water and cook at a light boil for 10 or 15 minutes. Add the wine, cook for another 5 or 10 minutes and leave to cool until tepid.

Prick the sausage on all sides with the point of a trussing needle, immerse it in the court-bouillon and bring to a near boil. Cover with the lid slightly ajar and regulate the heat to keep the court-bouillon beneath the boil; it should cook at about 85°C (185°F). Poach the sausage for 45 to 50 minutes.

Serve, sliced, with some of its court-bouillon ladled over, surrounded by little new potatoes boiled in salted water.

Truffled Sausage with Pistachios in Court-Bouillon

PIG'S TROTTERS AND CABBAGE

BRAISED IN BEAUJOLAIS

INGREDIENTS
METRIC AND IMPERIAL

4 pig's trotters

1 thick slice green (unsmoked) bacon, weighing about 225 g (8 oz), cut crosswise into 8 sections

1 tbsp olive oil

450 g (1 lb) carrots, cut into sections

450 g (1 lb) onions, coarsely chopped

3 garlic cloves, thinly sliced

large pinch of mixed dried herbs

salt

1 large fresh bouquet garni comprising 2 bay leaves, thyme, parsley or parsley root, lovage or celery and leek greens

about 1 bottle of red wine

1 large green cabbage

Serves 4

*Pig's Trotters and Cabbage
Braised in Beaujolais*

Best results will be had with an earthenware vessel – *pot-au-feu* or *daubière*. If using a gas flame, protect it from direct contact with an asbestos mat or other heat disperser.

Immerse the pig's trotters in a pan of cold water, bring slowly to the boil and drain, then rinse in cold water. Set aside.

Over low heat, cook the bacon pieces in the olive oil until lightly coloured. Add the carrots, onions and garlic, sprinkle with herbs and salt and cook, stirring from time to time, until the vegetables are softened and have begun to colour lightly. Remove the bacon pieces and put them aside. Place the trotters and the bouquet garni on the bed of vegetables and pour over red wine to cover. Bring to the boiling point and braise, covered, at a bare simmer for about 3 hours.

Meanwhile, quarter the cabbage and cut out the core. Remove any large ribs, then slice the cabbage coarsely. Parboil in a large pan of water for a few minutes until semi-tender. Drain in a colander, refresh under cold running water, and squeeze dry in handfuls.

Remove the trotters to a platter. Pour the contents of the pot into a large sieve, collecting the juices in a bowl. Discard the bouquet garni and empty the vegetables into another bowl. Leave the juices to settle until all the fat can be removed from the surface and discarded.

Make a bed with half the cabbage in the bottom of the pot, place the trotters on top and scatter around the pieces of bacon and the vegetables. Tuck in the remaining cabbage, packing it lightly, and pour over the braising juices. Braise covered, at a bare simmer, for another 2 hours or slightly more.

Serve directly from the cooking utensil, if the shape permits, or pile the contents on to a large, deep platter.

MACEDOINE OF FRUITS IN BEAUJOLAIS

Choose at least three or four fruits: peaches, skinned and sliced (if the skins resist, drop the peaches into boiling water and drain immediately); pears, peeled, cored and diced; strawberries; raspberries; grapes, skinned and seeded; cherries … Citrus fruits and pineapple do not mingle well with wine; peeled and sliced kiwi fruit is pretty but not especially flavourful. Instead of including whole raspberries, a few may be puréed and poured over the other fruits before the wine is added.

Mix the fruits together in a large glass bowl, sprinkle with sugar to taste and leave for a few minutes until the sugar has melted and penetrated the fruits. Pour over wine to cover. This is best prepared 1 to 2 hours in advance and refrigerated with a tight cover of plastic film.

INGREDIENTS
METRIC AND IMPERIAL

a selection of 3 or 4 fruits (see recipe)

caster sugar to taste

red wine to cover

Serves 4

Macédoine of Fruits in Beaujolais

Côtes du Rhône

The northern Rhône valley is Syrah country. In this 70 km (43 mile) stretch of vineyards, reaching from Vienne to Valence, no other red grape is grown. On the sheer, mountainous inclines of the Côte Rôtie and Hermitage, where no mechanisation is possible, the union of granitic soils and the Syrah grape produces massive, explosive wines; those of Cornas are not far behind in weight and in beauty. All are usually described as aggressive, hard, bitter, acrid, astringent... when young.

All of these unpleasant adjectives may apply; it is certain that these wines need a number of years to acquire good manners and longer for the aristocratic breeding to emerge. Four or five years after the vintage these wines are likely to be temporarily dumb, with only the hardness apparent. When still in the wood or within a couple of years after bottling, the freshness and density of the wild fruit and the intensity of the characteristic wine scent, defined as violets by the experts (I have never discovered it in the violets from my garden), mask the tannic presence; very young, after the first shock, a mouthful of Syrah dynamite is exhilarating.

Amongst the Côte Rôtie growers in whom one may have confidence are Robert Jasmin, Marius Gentaz, René Rostaing, Bernard Burgaud.... In Cornas, Auguste Clape, Noël Verset. In Hermitage, Gérard Chave, whose labels still bear the name of his father, Jean-Louis Chave, as well as the legend, 'Vignerons from father to son since 1481', is a friend and one could hope for no better wine than his; to furnish my own cellar, I have never searched farther afield. In restaurants, I have often drunk with pleasure Paul Jaboulet's Hermitage 'La Chapelle'.

By providential coincidence, Kermit Lynch, an importer of wines to America, who is writing a book on wines and the growers with whom he works, rang up

BRAISED LAMB SHOULDER WITH A
RED HERMITAGE

Apéritif: Saint-Joseph blanc

Seafood Salad with Saffron Cream Sauce
CONDRIEU

Stuffed, Braised Lamb Shoulder, White Purée
HERMITAGE (JEAN-LOUIS CHAVE)
1 9 8 1

Cheeses
COTE ROTIE
(older than the Hermitage)

Peaches in Red Crozes-Hermitage

while I was writing the paragraphs above to say that he was working on his northern Rhône chapter and would like my thoughts about the differences between Hermitage and Cornas. He had taken notes at a discussion held with Gérard Chave and Auguste Clape. Their conclusions were pretty much the same: Cornas is a rougher, more rustic wine, which seems even harder – more tannic – in youth and is slow to reveal itself but, after seven or eight years, begins to open up with a self-contained, majestic poise that is awesome; Hermitage has greater elegance and dimension and, at the same time, reveals its depth and potential more precociously.

Condrieu and the single property appellation, Château Grillet, both just south of Vienne and the Côte Rôtie, are planted with the white Viognier grape, believed by some to have arrived in France 2,600 years ago with the Phocaean Greeks. It is grown in no other region. Up to 20% Viognier is authorised, in combination with Syrah, for the red Côte Rôtie – no white wine is made there. Wine writers discover honey, peaches, almonds and acacia blossom in the smell and taste of Condrieu. It is best drunk young while its fruit is fresh.

Except for Condrieu and Château Grillet, all white wines in the northern Côtes du Rhône are made predominantly from the Marsanne grape in combination with varying proportions of Roussanne. White Hermitage has a skeleton of steel and deserves to be laid down for several years before being drunk; depending on the vintage, it will continue to evolve for many years or many decades. I have, several times, tasted back through vintages in Chave's cellars to the 1929s, both red and white, both in perfect condition after six decades. The 1929 white is stamped in the transcendental white wine corner of my memory along with the 1966 Montrachet from the Domaine de la Romanée Conti and the 1921 Yquem. 1947 and 1967 are amongst the other startling vintages.

Saint-Joseph, across the river from Hermitage, stretches the length of the right bank from Condrieu to Cornas. The wine is mostly red, in a lighter vein than the giants mentioned above and, at best, extremely seductive when drunk within a few years of the vintage; the same is true of the whites. Raymond Trollat, Jean-Louis Grippat and Gérard Chave make fine Saint-Joseph; Chave's is practically unfindable. Saint-Péray, to the south of Cornas, is all white, mostly sparkling; a few growers make some still Saint-Péray.

Crozes-Hermitage, by far the largest appellation area, imposes the same kind of confusion as that created by the Côte d'Or, where the names of the villages have incorporated the names of the greatest growths. Crozes-Hermitage is on the left bank, the same grape varieties are grown there to make both red and white wines; but for these similarities, Crozes-Hermitage has nothing to do with Hermitage. Good, satisfying wines are made from grapes grown on the hillsides; Crozes-Hermitage from the plain is of indifferent quality.

Most of these wines, both reds and whites, have a powerful resistance to aggression, although one should take care not to bring violent flavours to a Condrieu (I hesitated before using saffron in the salad, but it works). The reds are very much at home with the kind of dish in which many elements, through long braising, meld into a single, subtle and complex flavour; the lamb shoulder is an example, and the duck from the Jura menu or the oxtail in the menu from the south-west would be equally well served by one of these reds. The big reds are perfect companions to game birds – grouse or woodcock – or a rare roast saddle of hare (or hare fillets, encrusted with chopped truffles and sweated, with butter and a sprinkling of Cognac, for seven or eight minutes).

TIMING

Prepare the peaches the previous day or hours ahead, seal with plastic film and refrigerate. The lamb's shoulder may be stuffed and tied up ahead of time – the previous day and refrigerated, if desired. It will require about two and a half hours in all from the time it is put into the oven to be seared. It can't be hurried, but it can be held. It is probably easiest to finish the glazing and hold it in a warm place before going to table. The fish should not be prepared so far in advance that it has to be refrigerated (even if brought back to room temperature the delicacy of the flavours will have been lost through refrigeration); it is best still tepid or at room temperature. Except for the last-minute assemblage of the salad, the preparations can be begun as soon as the shoulder is put into the oven. The vegetables for the purée can be put to cook about 15 minutes before the end of the shoulder's braising time, before it is put to glaze; they can be puréed and kept covered in a warm place before being finished at the last minute.

SEAFOOD SALAD
WITH SAFFRON CREAM SAUCE

INGREDIENTS
METRIC AND IMPERIAL

900 g (2 lb) fresh mussels

sea salt

1 onion, finely chopped

1 garlic clove, crushed

sprig of thyme

bay leaf

about 125 ml (4 fl oz) white wine

6 fresh scallops, cleaned

2 small squid, cleaned

100 g (4 oz) firm button
   mushrooms

juice of ½ lemon

100 g (4 oz) small mange-tout
   peas, topped and tailed

handful of decorative salad leaves
   such as oak leaf lettuce, lamb's
   lettuce, rocket etc.

FOR THE SAUCE

knife tip of powdered saffron

pinch of saffron threads

salt and freshly ground pepper

juice of 1 lemon

125 ml (4 fl oz) double cream

FOR THE GARNISH

wild fennel leaves and chopped
   chives – or dill or tarragon
   alone

Serves 4

Sole fillets, cut into strips on the bias, or large prawns or shrimp, shelled raw, can replace the mussels in this salad. The chopped up sole carcass or the prawn shells provide a little stock (white wine, water, chopped onion, thyme, bay) in which the sole strips or prawns are poached in the same way as the scallops.

The mushroom stems can be used elsewhere for making a duxelles or flavouring a sauce; if you have no other use for them, chop them up and throw them in with the mussels to add flavour to the liquid.

The scallops are poached whole and sliced later because they lose fewer juices and, when sliced, the interior remains a pristine white. Squid, to be tender, requires either a flash contact with heat, as here, or a prolonged braising treatment as in the Loire Valley menu.

To clean the mussels, first discard any with broken shells, then soak in a basin of water with a handful of sea salt for 15 or 20 minutes: as they yawn, they will discharge much of the sand contained in their shells. (Cultivated mussels contain no sand and need no cleaning except for a rapid rinse.) Pull out the beards, brush the mussels and rinse them.

Combine the mussels, onion, garlic, herbs and wine in a large saucepan, cover and place over high heat. Shake the saucepan repeatedly and, when the mussels begin to open, remove from the heat. Transfer the opened mussels to a dish; return the others to the heat, continuing to shake the covered pan. When most are opened, pour the lot into a colander placed over a bowl. Remove the mussels from their shells, collecting them in a small bowl (it is always written that any mussels that do not open should be discarded; it is my experience that those which resist opening are, when pried open, the most succulent – use your discretion). Spoon over enough of their cooking liquid to keep them moist and put them aside. Carefully pour the remainder of the liquid through a sieve lined with a couple of layers of moistened and wrung-out muslin or cheesecloth, stopping when sediment appears in the bottom of the bowl.

Place the scallops in a small saucepan that just holds them, side by side, and pour over the cooled mussels' liquid. Bring to a near boil, covered, over moderate to low heat. Remove from the heat before the boil is reached and leave them to poach, covered, until opaque and firm to the touch. Remove the scallops with a slotted spoon and put aside.

Split the squid tentacles in two at the base, and cut the body pouch into thin rings. Bring the scallop/mussel cooking liquid to a rapid boil. Add the squid tentacles and rings, give them a swirl and a stir and, before the liquid returns to the boil, pour them into a sieve, collecting the juices in a bowl underneath. Put the squid tentacles and rings aside.

Return the juices to the pan and reduce over moderate heat until slightly thickened and only 2 or 3 tablespoons remain. Add the saffron powder and threads. Transfer to a bowl and leave to cool. Taste the reduction for salt, add more if necessary, and add pepper and about half the lemon juice. Stir in the cream, then taste again for salt and lemon, adjusting the seasoning to taste. Set aside.

Slice off the mushroom stems at the base of the cap, then rinse the caps rapidly and dry them in a towel. Slice thinly, vertically, and toss with the lemon juice to keep them white.

Remove any strings from the mange-tout and slice each one once or twice on the bias. Parboil in boiling salted water for a few seconds and drain.

When ready to assemble the salad, drain the mussels and slice the scallops, across the grain, into two or three slices each. Combine the two with the squid and about half the sauce. Line a platter with the salad leaves. Scatter over the sauced seafood, the mushrooms and mange-tout, spoon over the remaining sauce and sprinkle with fresh herbs.

Seafood Salad with Saffron Cream Sauce

STUFFED, BRAISED LAMB SHOULDER

INGREDIENTS
METRIC AND IMPERIAL

1 shoulder of lamb, boned and as much fat as possible removed

olive oil

salt

coarsely chopped mirepoix (page 18), based on 2 carrots and 1 large onion

about 250 ml (8 fl oz) white wine

stock (page 18), made from the bones, any lamb or veal trimmings available and, if desired, chicken wings or wingtips

FOR THE STUFFING

large handful (about 90 g/3½ oz) of semi-fresh breadcrumbs

about 50 g (2 oz) green (unsmoked) bacon, finely diced or chopped

persillade (page 15)

1 egg

pinch of mixed dried herbs

salt and freshly ground pepper

Serves 4

When boning a lamb shoulder, butchers usually tunnel out the middle bone, corresponding to the upper arm. If this is done, slice through the flesh the length of the tunnel to open it out. The boned shoulder, laid out skin side down, presents an irregular, squarish, star-like shape. If you want to bone it yourself, feel your way, using a small, sharply pointed knife and always working against the bone. Get rid of the shoulder blade first, opening out flaps of flesh to expose its entire surface from joint to outside edge. When the joint is severed at the socket and scraped or cut clean at the tip, it can be pulled backward, the membrane which separates the flesh from the underside, rudder-shaped blade's surface, clinging to the flesh; if you get off to a bad start, the membrane will cling to the bone and the flesh will tear. In that case, you will have to continue scraping with the knife tip. The other two bones can be removed together. Cut down to the middle bone from joint to joint and scrape the flesh free from the shank bone up to the joint; the flesh is easily separated the length of the bones – only the cartilage and tendons at the joints offer resistance. You will have to feel your way around a little wing-like protrusion at the joint of the shank bone.

Mix together the stuffing ingredients until they form a coherent mass (if there is not enough moisture to pull them together, add a few drops of olive oil). Pack the stuffing into all the crevices of the shoulder, laid out flat, so that flesh and stuffing form a smooth-surfaced mound. Run a trussing needle and kitchen string through two more or less opposed corners of the shoulder, pull them together and tie, then repeat with two other corners or protrusions in the contour to form a purse shape. Tie the shoulder up, encircling it from top to bottom four times, with the strings crossing at top centre and bottom centre, to create a melon shape of eight sections. Use several lengths of string if this seems easier.

Preheat the oven to 200°C (400°F or Mark 6).

Rub the surface of the lamb with a few drops of olive oil, sprinkle with salt and place in a small, round roasting pan or heavy frying pan. Roast for 35 to 40 minutes or until nicely coloured golden.

Make a bed of mirepoix in a round, heavy saucepan or cocotte of a size just to hold the shoulder at ease, and place the shoulder on top. Discard the fat from the roasting pan, deglaze with some of the white wine and pour this liquid over the lamb, along with the rest of the wine and enough stock to immerse by two-thirds or three-quarters, more or less. Bring to a near boil, adjust to a bare simmer and cook, covered, for about 1½ hours.

Remove the shoulder to a plate. Clip and carefully remove the strings (if it were left tied, the glaze would be damaged in removing them later) and return it to the roasting pan originally used for searing in the oven. Strain the juices into a small saucepan, pressing the mirepoix to extract all liquid before discarding it. Remove as much fat as possible from the surface of the juices after they have settled a bit, then spoon enough over the shoulder to coat the bottom of the roasting pan. Put it into a preheated 190°C (375°F or Mark 5) oven.

Bring the juices remaining in the saucepan to the boil. Pull the pan half off the heat and adjust to maintain a light boil on one side of the liquid's surface. Regularly skim off the skin of fatty impurities that forms on the still side of the surface. At the same time, baste the shoulder regularly, taking a small ladle of liquid from the boiling side of the reducing juices when there is no longer enough in the roasting pan. After about half an hour, the shoulder will be coated in a rich, deep caramel glaze and the remaining juices in the saucepan should be completely fat-free and of a light syrupy consistency.

Carve in wedges, with the sauce served separately.

Stuffed, Braised Lamb Shoulder and White Purée with a red Hermitage

WHITE PUREE

INGREDIENTS
METRIC AND IMPERIAL

400 g (14 oz) tender, crisp turnips, peeled and quartered if large

unsalted butter for cooking

1 medium celeriac, peeled and cut into large cubes

salt

400 g (14 oz) onions, quartered if large

400 g (14 oz) potatoes, peeled and cut up according to size

1 head of garlic, cloves separated and peeled

about 100 g (4 oz) butter, cut into small pieces

Serves 4

It was my intention to serve a yellow purée with the Stuffed, Braised Lamb Shoulder, using swedes instead of turnips, mostly because the colour is so lovely; both purées are delicious. But there were no swedes in the market.

A turnip's structure holds water when cooked, so here the turnips are cooked in butter after parboiling to dry them out, to prevent the purée from being too thin.

The cooking liquid is delicious – rich enough to serve on its own as a soup. It is also a sumptuous stock for use as a minestrone base or to moisten a ragoût. Don't discard it.

As usual, precise proportions are of no interest. A medium celeriac weighs about 400 g (14 oz) and, except for the garlic, the vegetables should be more or less equal in quantity.

Parboil the turnips in a large pan of water until semi-tender, then drain and cook over a low heat in butter for about 30 minutes, shaking or tossing regularly.

Meanwhile, add the celeriac to a pan of boiling salted water and, about 15 minutes later, add the onions, potatoes and garlic. Cook at a light boil until all the vegetables are tender, about 30 minutes longer. Drain in a colander.

With the turnips, pass the vegetables, in portions, through a large, fine sieve, pushing them through with a wooden pestle (a food mill will make a coarser but acceptable purée; however, do not use an electric processor). Return the purée to the saucepan and reheat over medium to high heat, stirring rapidly and constantly with a wooden spoon to prevent sticking. Remove from the heat and add the butter, continuing to stir until it is absorbed.

PEACHES IN RED CROZES-HERMITAGE

Dunk the peaches in boiling water, drain them immediately and then peel them.

In a stainless steel saucepan or, preferably, an untinned copper jam pan or copper bowl for whisking egg whites, bring the peaches, sugar and wine to the boil. Cook at a very light boil until the peaches are tender to the prodding of a trussing needle. Remove them to a plate. With the heat a bit higher, reduce the liquid to a syrupy consistency. The time necessary for this reduction depends on the size and shape of the cooking vessel; when the boiling begins to make a slurring sound the syrupy degree should be right.

Pour the red wine syrup over the peaches in a bowl and, when cooled, cover and refrigerate. The parts of the peaches that are immersed in the syrup will turn a dark red, whereas those remaining above the surface are paler; for this reason, it is best to turn them around in their syrup a couple of times and to set them up in their presentation dish only at the last moment, deep red surfaces up, syrup freshly poured over.

INGREDIENTS
METRIC AND IMPERIAL

8 yellow peaches

150 g (5 oz) sugar

1 bottle of red Crozes-Hermitage or other decent red wine

Serves 4

Peaches in Red Crozes-Hermitage

THE SOUTHERN COTES DU RHONE AND

The southern Côtes du Rhône wines come from the heart of Provence, none of them very far from Avignon. The best known and the most interesting is Châteauneuf-du-Pape, the largest single *appellation contrôlée* in France. Less than two per cent of the production is white wine, the remainder red. Thirteen grape varieties, including several white, are permitted in red Châteauneuf-du-Pape but, as there is no legislation concerning proportions, it is possible to produce Châteauneuf-du-Pape with Grenache alone. Château de Beaucastel has all 13; most growers limit themselves to five or six varieties with Grenache dominating and Cinsault, Mourvèdre and Syrah recurring most often; Clairette, a white grape, is often present also. Châteauneuf takes age well and eventually develops a rich, gamey bouquet, making it a classic partner to civet de lièvre, a red wine and hare stew finished with the hare's blood.

To acquire a full, sensory picture of Châteauneuf-du-Pape, travellers in the south of France can do no better than to take a few meals at Hiély in Avignon, perhaps the most interesting restaurant in France for quality and good value as well as for the beauty of its wine list. A dozen growers from Châteauneuf and as many vintages – some 35 Châteauneufs in all, including seven or eight whites – are listed. A magnum of Domaine de Mont-Redon 1961, recently drunk there, was spectacular. A supple, tender and fruity red Châteauneuf, vinified especially for Pierre Hiély, to be drunk in the year following the vintage, is served cool in pitchers.

Gigondas makes rather rough, solidly built wines from the same grape varieties as Châteauneuf-du-Pape. A host of other wine areas from the southern Rhône valley – Côtes du Rhône, Côtes du Rhône-Villages, more than a

LAMB BROCHETTES, CHEESE AND A
BANDOL WINE

Apéritif: Châteauneuf-du-Pape blanc or Cassis blanc

Courgette and Tomato Tart
CHATEAU SIMONE (PALETTE)
BLANC

Brochettes of Lamb Parts in Caul,
Pilaf with Spring Vegetables
DOMAINE TEMPIER (BANDOL)
ROUGE 1984

Cheeses
DOMAINE DU VIEUX TELEGRAPHE
(CHATEAUNEUF-DU-PAPE) 1982

Gratin of Fresh Figs
MUSCAT DE BEAUMES-DE-VENISE

dozen Côtes du Rhône hyphenated with the name of a village, Côtes du Ventoux, Coteaux du Tricastin and Lirac – nearly all make red, white and rosé wines, inexpensive and easy to drink in their youth. Tavel is all rosé. Muscat de Beaumes-de-Venise is amber and sweet.

The Provence of wine appellations stretches from Marseilles to Nice, never far from the Mediterranean coast. Until about ten years ago, when *appellation contrôlée* rights were bestowed upon the widely dispersed vineyards of the Côtes de Provence (to appease hurt feelings, it is said, after a number of Corsican wines had been thus honoured), there were only four vineyard areas which enjoyed that distinction: Palette, a stone's throw from Aix-en-Provence, the outlying regions of Cassis and Bandol (small fishing ports on the coast between Marseilles and Toulon) and Bellet, in the suburban hills of Nice.

Almost the entire Palette appellation is absorbed by the 17 hectares (40 acres) of Château Simone; a high proportion of the vines are very old – 50 years or more – with a naturally low production; the proprietor, René Rougier, is proud of vinifying his wines in the same way as did his father and his grandfather. The red wine, composed of the same principal grape varieties as that from Châteauneuf, remains for two years in large oak tuns and passes its third year in barrels before bottling; it is at its best after at least four or five years of bottle age. The rosé, which passes a year in wood, has a closer affinity to red wine than most rosés. Two types of white wine are bottled: they are the same wine, made predominantly from small-grained Clairette, a mixture of other traditional Provençal white varieties and a minuscule proportion of Muscat. One, labelled *blanc de blancs*, bottled a few months after the vintage, is pale with green glints, fresh and floral and is best drunk young with all that freshness intact; the other, bottled after two or three years, depending on the vintage, bronzed from its evolution in the wood, continues to evolve in complexity and is lovely when drunk ten or fifteen years old. At the château, the precocious bottling is served, in the year following the vintage, as an apéritif and the old-fashioned white, often several vintages of it, is served at table.

Red and rosé are made at Cassis but it is the sturdy, uncomplicated white, which easily supports the assault of Provençal seasoning, on which its reputation is based. In Marseilles, nearly all bouillabaisse and bourrides are washed down with Cassis. Bellet is made in such small quantities that it is nearly all portioned out amongst the fashionable restaurants in and around Nice.

The wines of Bandol come from the hillsides of several communities; the slopes form a semi-circular basin or natural amphitheatre with the village of Bandol standing stage-centre, a surrounding chain of mountains creating a protective wind-breaker and the proximity of the sea conferring summer coolness and winter warmth. During the eighteenth and nineteenth centuries, Bandol was an important wine-shipping port: its red wines were known for solidity and longevity, for which the Mourvèdre grape must claim a good part of the credit. After the decimation of the vineyards by phylloxera in the last half of the nineteenth century, Mourvèdre, a late ripener and low producer, was not replanted and the wine's reputation dwindled. When the appellation was consecrated in 1941, legislation imposed a minimum of 10% Mourvèdre. Lucien Peyraud, proprietor of Domaine Tempier, has for 40 years led a crusade under the Mourvèdre banner; today red Bandol must contain a minimum of 50% Mourvèdre. Domaine Tempier averages 70% Mourvèdre, which, in combination with Cinsault, Grenache and a smattering of Syrah, produces an astonishing wine infused with all the scents of Provence, the fruit of wild berries and the capacity to age gracefully for several decades. From the same grape varieties, but with a smaller proportion of Mourvèdre, Tempier also makes a lovely rosé which, because of its good-natured propensity for bringing people together in happy communion, my friend Kermit Lynch, in his wine brochures, has characterised as 'the best wine in the world'.

The table at Domaine Tempier is a continuing celebration of Provence and Bandol. Lulu (Madame Peyraud, née Tempier) haunts the local fishing ports to choose lunch from the night's catch as the boats arrive early in the morning. Lunch often opens with a huge platter of sea urchins and *violets*, the leathery little sea-floor creatures commonly eaten on the coast between Marseilles and Toulon, which, when cut open, reveal a delicate, lemon-coloured flesh; it always opens with the most recently bottled Tempier rosé (although, like many vignerons who serve their own wines at table, Lucien often serves Champagne as an apéritif), followed by several vintages of Tempier red, whether the main course be fish or meat.

The last time I visited, for this book, Lulu had returned

with stiff-arched, bright-eyed sardines glinting steely blue, a sign that they are fresh from the fishing nets, the largest gurnard that I have ever seen and a giant bream, *lou pagre*, the most admired of Mediterranean breams, always designated by its magisterial Provençal name. After tasting several *cuvées* of the 1985s and 1984s in the cellars, we sat down to this Provençal menu:

FRITURE DE COURGETTES ET D'ARTICHAUTS

(Sliced courgettes and artichoke hearts, floured and fried in olive oil)

DOMAINE TEMPIER ROSE 1985

FILETS DE SARDINES CRUS, SAUCE CRUE A LA TOMATE

(Raw sardine fillets, sprinkled with lemon juice, seasoned, dribbled with olive oil, uncooked sauce of peeled, seeded, chopped tomatoes, finely diced onion and olive oil)

DOMAINE TEMPIER 1983

LE GRONDIN ET LOU PAGRE AU FOUR

(Fish seasoned and covered with rows of lemon slices, surrounded with branches of herbs, baked and basted with olive oil and white wine)

HERBES AU GRATIN A LA PROVENÇALE

(Swiss chard, sorrel and lettuce, parboiled, squeezed and chopped, cooked long and gently in butter with a sprinkling of flour, milk added as it is absorbed; turned into a buttered gratin dish, sprinkled with breadcrumbs, shavings of butter and baked in a slow oven for about an hour)

DOMAINE TEMPIER 1971

FROMAGES

(Reblochon, Comté and fresh local goat cheeses)

DOMAINE TEMPIER 1968

PANIER DE FRUITS FRAIS

(Fresh fruits)

TIMING

The tart is better tepid than hot from the oven; it should be put to bake an hour before going to table. The brochettes, except for grilling, may be prepared in advance; it is easier not to prepare them more than an hour or so ahead of time, which eliminates the necessity of refrigerating them and then removing them from the refrigerator far enough in advance to bring them back to room temperature before grilling. The pilaf should be begun at the same time that the tart is served. The figs may be peeled, halved and laid out in their dish, covered with plastic film and refrigerated two or three hours in advance, if desired.

COURGETTE AND TOMATO TART

For the beauty of the presentation, the slices of tomato should remain intact and undeformed. To peel the tomatoes, use a small, sharply pointed paring knife, cut out a cone at the stem end of each to remove the core, then slit a cross in the skin at the bottom or flower end and plunge them into a pot of boiling water. Drain immediately and slip off the skins, pulling the corners at the cross, between thumb and knife blade, toward the stem ends. To seed the tomatoes, slice each in half horizontally or crosswise, delicately loosen the pockets of seeds with the tip of your little finger and shake gently to get rid of seeds and water. Slice thickly crosswise (you should get four perfect slices from each tomato – use the end slices or any damaged slices in a salad or a sauce). Generously sprinkle both sides of each slice with salt and lay out the slices on a large, overturned nylon drum sieve (or, lacking that, on a pastry grill first covered with a tea towel) to drain. They will lose a lot of water which would otherwise interfere with the correct cooking of the custard. After half an hour, they may be sponged gently dry, either with a tea towel or between paper towels.

While the tomatoes are being salted, prepare the courgettes. Grate them through the medium blade of a mouli-julienne or food processor, then layer them in a bowl, salting the layers, and leave to drain for 15 to 30 minutes. Squeeze dry to a firm ball. Sauté the courgettes in the butter for a few minutes to cook them slightly and further dry them out.

Preheat the oven to 180°–190°C (350°–375°F or Mark 4–5).

Scatter the courgettes loosely over the bottom of the tart shell. Lay the tomato slices symmetrically on top, barely touching each other, and place a slice of cheese on each tomato. Whisk together the cream, eggs and seasoning and ladle evenly over the contents of the tart shell. Bake for 30 to 40 minutes or until swelled and golden.

INGREDIENTS
METRIC AND IMPERIAL

3 large tomatoes, weighing about 450 g (1 lb) in total
salt
450 g (1 lb) small firm courgettes
15 g (½ oz) unsalted butter
1 deep 25 cm (10 in) tart shell, baked blind (page 20)
90 g (3½ oz) Gruyère cheese, cut into thin squares
500 ml (16 fl oz) double cream
4 eggs
freshly ground pepper

Serves 4

Courgette and Tomato Tart, before the addition of the egg and cream mixture

BROCHETTES OF LAMB PARTS IN CAUL

INGREDIENTS
METRIC AND IMPERIAL

2 lamb's hearts

4 lamb's kidneys

225 g (8 oz) lamb's liver, cut into 12 cubes

persillade (page 15)

large pinch of mixed dried herbs

several spring onions, tender green parts included, sliced very thinly, or 1 small onion, peeled and finely chopped

salt and freshly ground pepper

about 2 tbsp olive oil

caul

Serves 4

Choose – or ask your butcher to choose – pale-coloured kidneys. Dark, reddish-brown kidneys are always strong-flavoured; pale rose-beige-coloured kidneys are delicately flavoured. If any of these meats are unavailable, substitute calf's liver or kidney, sweetbreads, pre-prepared as for braising, or pieces of lean lamb fillet or top of the leg.

Caul is not only a nourisher and, as the threads of fat melt to golden-brown lace, a beautiful dressing, but it is a container which holds everything in place, preventing, in this instance, the chopped onions of the marinade from falling into the embers and flaming up (when I prepare brochettes without caul, I eliminate also the chopped onions). Caul is often used to wrap up split and flattened quail or other small meats that have been coated with mirepoix or duxelles. If using salted or frozen caul, soak it in tepid water until it is supple.

If you have neither a fireplace nor a barbecue and no possibility of building a fire on the ground out-of-doors, place the brochettes on an oven tray and grill them.

Parts of the hillside where I live are a jungle of wild rosemary. Twenty-five years ago, I tore up quantities of seedlings and planted them to hedge around the terrace which is my garden so I am never lacking in disposable brochettes. If available, use 30 cm (1 ft) lengths of stiff branch, tufts of leaves left at one end, the branches scraped smooth and sharpened to a point at the other end. Save the leaves that you have pulled off to throw on to the embers a few seconds before removing the brochettes from the grill; the smoke of smouldering fresh rosemary is a wonderful seasoning. The best grill is made of heavy, welded iron bars and should be preheated for 5 or 10 minutes before use.

To prepare the hearts, trim them of surface fat and connecting tubes, split them and rinse to rid them of clotted blood. Cut them into 6 or 8 equal-sized chunks.

Remove the membranes from the kidneys, then cut each into three sections crosswise.

Combine all the ingredients, except the caul, in a mixing bowl and toss with your hands until all meats are evenly coated with the marinade elements. Alternate the meats, piercing them on the rosemary branches or skewers, so that they touch but are not packed. Start and finish with a piece of heart which is the firmest meat and will hold the others in place. Roll each skewer into a rectangle of caul, first spooning over leftover marinade and chopped onions; twist the caul at each end of the skewered meats to seal.

Grill for 10 to 15 minutes, or about 3 minutes on each side (four sides). The meats should remain pink or medium rare to be tender and juicy; if overcooked, they are dry and tough.

Opposite: The Lamb Brochettes on the fire

PILAF WITH SPRING VEGETABLES

In a heavy saucepan, over low heat, cook the onion in the oil until softened but not coloured. Add the rice and a little salt and cook for 2 or 3 minutes, stirring from time to time, until the rice is coated with the oil and has turned slightly milky or more opaque. Pour in the boiling water, cover tightly and cook over very low heat, at a slight simmer, for about 18 minutes or until all the water is absorbed.

Meanwhile, prepare the garnish. Parboil the beans in salted water for about 1 minute at a rolling boil, then drain. Cut the carrots lengthwise into slices, then into strips, and then cut crosswise into dice. Cook in water almost to cover with the sugar, butter and a pinch of salt for about 10 minutes or until the water has evaporated and the carrots are glazed.

Remove the rice from the heat, add the garnish and the diced butter and toss lightly with two forks until the grains of rice are separated and the garnish evenly distributed. Serve directly from the cooking utensil, or emptied on to a heated platter with the brochettes (page 60) atop.

Little peas or peeled, tender broad beans, rapidly parboiled, diced sweet red pepper or diced celery heart, sweated in a little olive oil or butter, or a peeled, seeded, chopped tomato, tossed in olive oil over high heat for a few seconds, are other garnish possibilities.

INGREDIENTS
METRIC AND IMPERIAL

1 medium onion, finely chopped
1 tbsp olive oil
225 g (8 oz) long-grain rice
salt
500 ml (16 fl oz) boiling water
25 g (1 oz) cold butter, diced

FOR THE GARNISH

about 65 g (2½ oz) small green beans, cut crosswise into 5 mm (¼ in) lengths (the size of little peas)
about 65 g (2½ oz) carrots
pinch of sugar
dab of unsalted butter

Serves 4

GRATIN OF FRESH FIGS

Green or blackish-purple-skinned autumn figs with deep red flesh are much better than the bland, yellowish-pink-fleshed summer figs, and they are much the best when picked ripe from the tree at the moment that filigree cracks begin to appear on the skin's surface.

If only liquid cream is available, omit it.

Choose a gratin dish into which the half figs may be placed, side by side, touching, cut surfaces facing up. Pour in only enough water to create a film on the bottom of the dish, then arrange the figs on top. Dribble a few drops of Chartreuse over the surface of each, then probably about ½ teaspoon of honey on each (impossible to measure because of its lazy flow). Add a small dab, perhaps another ½ teaspoon, of stiff cream on top. Place beneath very high heat (or, preferably, in an oven or salamander with heat sources both above and below) for 4 or 5 minutes, or until the surfaces and the liquids in the bottom of the dish are bubbling.

INGREDIENTS
METRIC AND IMPERIAL

about 12 figs, peeled and split in two

1–2 tbsp water

green Chartreuse liqueur

liquid honey, preferably lavender or thyme

2–3 tbsp stiff double cream

Serves 4

Gratin of Fresh Figs

ROBUST SIMPLICTY
FROM THE

South West

Gathered together here under a blanket heading are several regions. Those of the Languedoc and Roussillon, which follow the Mediterranean coast to the Spanish border, use mainly the same grape varieties which go into the wines of the southern Rhône and Provence. Costières du Gard, south of Nîmes, resembles the generic Côtes du Rhône wines and could as well have been included amongst the wines of Provence.

The vast quantities of indifferent wine made in the Languedoc, used for blending anonymous red table wines, have given the region an undeservedly bad reputation. Lovely, clean, refreshing wines are made there which, in terms of a quality-price relationship, are surely the greatest bargains in France. Two of these, both Corbières and both best drunk within the year following the vintage, I have chosen to highlight because they have given me so much pleasure at so little cost in recent years.

Each proprietor has indulged in a bit of fantasy on his label to glamorise the wine. The white is labelled *blanc de blancs*, white wine made from white grapes; this means nothing outside Champagne, where a large proportion of the white wines are made by rapidly pressing red Pinot noir grapes to draw off the colourless juice of the pulp, untainted by the pigment contained in the skins (elsewhere all white wines are made from white grapes). But for many consumers, the term *blanc de blancs* carries implications of elegance associated with Champagne. The rosé is an authentic *vin gris*, which simply means a very pale rosé wine: the label reads *gris de gris*, which should mean grey (pale pink) wine made from grey grapes but, in fact, is merely a pretty name.

Côtes du Roussillon, mainly red, and the red Côtes du Roussillon-Villages are good daily table wines – firm, fruity and inexpensive. On the Mediterranean coast, near the Spanish border, the dense, sweet, fortified wines of Banyuls, usually drunk elsewhere as apéritif or after-

OXTAIL AND PIG'S EAR STEW WITH A CAHORS WINE

Apéritif: Vin blanc de Corbières, Roque Sestière
(Jean Bérail)

Braised Chicory
VIN GRIS DE CORBIERES,
DOMAINE DE FONTSAINTE
(Y. LABOUCARIE)

Oxtail and Pig's Ear Stew, Boiled Potatoes
CAHORS

Cheeses
MADIRAN

Honey-Glazed Apple Tart
JURANÇON *(liquoreux)*

dinner wines, are, in the region itself, often drunk at table. André Parcé proudly – and rightly – claims that Banyuls is one of the very rare wines that can be happily married to a chocolate dessert.

More to the centre, Cahors is thought to be the ideal accompaniment to cassoulet. Tradition claims it to be rough, black and tannic, requiring eight to ten years of bottle age before taming down. But a more supple wine is produced today, softened mainly by a discreet presence of the Merlot grape and a shorter maceration than before. It is still firm and uncomplicated, a fine accompaniment to rustic dishes robustly and complexly flavoured by the melding of many elements – cassoulets, daubes, estouffades, etc.

In the outlying regions to the east of Bordeaux a number of wines, good value and reminiscent of lesser Bordeaux, are made from the traditional Bordelais grape varieties – Cabernet-Sauvignon, Cabernet franc and Merlot for the reds; Sémillon, Sauvignon and Muscadelle for the whites. Amongst the better known appellations are Monbazillac (white and traditionally sweet, now often dry), Montravel (white), Bergerac (red and white), Côtes de Duras (red and white), Pécharmant (red) and Côte de Buzet (red, rosé and white).

Not far from the Spanish border and the Atlantic coast, Madiran owes its deep colour, rough texture and intensity to the Tannat grape. With a few years of age, it is a vigorous, satisfying wine, well suited to the hearty foods of the south-west. It is not much drunk outside the region, little exported and, like the Jurançon, its inclusion in the following menu is due to the faint hope that demand may bring it on to a larger market.

Jurançon is famous for having been the first liquid to brush the infant lips of Henri IV, later to become the first of the Bourbon kings of France. When made in the age-old manner, from grapes withered to raisins on the vines, it is also the most spectacular wine of the south-west (excluding Bordeaux): burnished gold, vibrant, nervous, liquorous, luscious – and a rarity. It needs age; the '47s are wonderful today.

Travellers in the south-west will find a large and varied choice of regional wines at André Daguin's Hôtel de France in Auch and all of the right foods, abundantly served, to accompany them.

One of the more irritating and imbecilic of the rules set down by the gastronomic law-makers pretends that vegetables, as such, are a detriment to the appreciation of wine. Anyone with common sense and a palate can disprove that by drinking the brisk rosé recommended here with the first course of braised chicory. This is not to say that the marriage between the chicory and rosé is so special that no other wine is possible. Because the dish is so simple – except for a couple of ritual gestures, it prepares itself – it is one of my stand-bys for solitary winter evenings when I am occupied with things other than cooking; depending on whim and, to a certain extent, on whether it serves as a first or a main course, I drink, with equal pleasure, a white or a pink Corbières, a Chinon or a red Bandol with it.

The Oxtail and Pig's Ear Stew is a perfect example of the melding and juxtaposition of multiple flavours and textures; it is best accompanied by a relatively young and robust but unassuming wine. It is exciting food but too demanding on the palate to permit the full appreciation of an old and delicate aristocrat from Burgundy or Bordeaux. The Madiran will support cheeses too strongly flavoured for most red wines and the apple tart will admirably throw into relief any luscious wine that is sweeter than the tart itself.

TIMING

The pastry should be fresh, but the tart may be prepared several hours in advance. The stew can be prepared the previous day and reheated if you like – in fact, little time is gained because, in order to prevent the meats sticking to the bottom of the cooking vessel the reheating must be pursued so gently that a couple of hours may be required to return the dish to a simmer. It should, in any case, be taken apart and reassembled – the sauce cleansed, reduced and poured back over the meats – then returned to low heat just before putting the chicory to cook, about 45 minutes before going to table. The pre-cooked garlic cloves should not be added too far in advance, lest they disintegrate in the sauce. The potatoes can be put to cook at the same time as, or just before, the chicory, then peeled and laid lightly on the stew's surface to keep hot during the first course.

BRAISED CHICORY

INGREDIENTS
METRIC AND IMPERIAL

15 g (½ oz) unsalted butter

*8 heads of chicory, blemished outer
leaves removed, bases (root
ends) trimmed, unwashed*

salt

*2–3 slices of prosciutto, cut into
narrow strips*

juice of 1 lemon

*100–125 ml (3–4 fl oz) double
cream*

Serves 4

Any number of little vegetable stews, each worthy of being
served as a course apart, can be created, singly or in combination, by sweating or braising the vegetables very gently with a
little butter or olive oil, tightly covered, in their own juices.
Some give less liquid than others and, with these, either a
chiffonade of lettuce added at the beginning or a dash of water
or white wine during cooking may be necessary to prevent
them from frying and sticking. Sweated in butter, they can be
finished off the heat by swirling in more butter or, as here, by
the addition of a bit of cream a minute before removing them
from the heat; in olive oil, they are often better finished with a
persillade (page 15) and a squeeze of lemon. Green vegetables
are an attractive addition to a mixed vegetable stew but,
because they do not like being overcooked, they are best either
pre-cooked apart – diced little green beans or broccoli florets,
their stems peeled and sliced, rapidly parboiled; thinly sliced

*Braised Chicory with a rosé wine
from Corbières*

and rapidly sautéed small courgettes – or raw (tiny peas, peeled little broad beans), and added a few minutes before removal from the heat.

One of my favourite mixed stews is made up of raw baby artichoke hearts, little onions, unpeeled garlic cloves, a bouquet garni and a chiffonade of lettuce, sweated for some 45 minutes, with a mess of peeled broad beans and some tender, chopped savory leaves thrown in a few minutes before removing from the heat and swirling in butter. But the choice of vegetables and herbs is dictated mainly by the seasons; little carrots, tiny crisp turnips, quartered bulbs of fennel, cauliflower florets and peeled or scraped little new potatoes are all possible elements. In another context, the chicory heads that are here braised whole can be sliced and scattered over a combination of vegetables in place of the lettuce chiffonade – or a chiffonade of sorrel, spinach or chard will do something very special.

Raw ham (prosciutto) is a thing that I always keep on hand to eat, depending on the season, with melon, figs, salads and other crudités for the kind of lunch that will not destroy an afternoon of work. Like many people, I take little pleasure in eating the abundant fat that surrounds the slices but it is a precious source of flavour and nourishment for many stews. Often I substitute slivered prosciutto fat for the ham called for in this recipe or, when in England or America, slivered bacon. The melody of the chicory's slight bitterness, the memory of meat, the sharpness of the lemon and the sweetness of the cream – and the velvety, subtly flavoured and beautifully coloured sauce drawn from only those elements – never fails to inspire wonder at the alchemical magic of the kitchen.

Smear the butter over the bottom of a large earthenware *poêlon* or heavy *sauteuse* of a size just to hold the chicory heads in a single layer. Fit them into place, sprinkle over salt and scatter over the strips of prosciutto. Cover tightly (if the lid does not fit tightly, first place a sheet of foil over the *poêlon* before putting the lid in place). Place over low heat, separated from the direct heat source by an asbestos pad or other heat disperser. After 20 minutes or so, when the chicory heads have coloured on one side, turn them over, taking care not to damage their shape. Cook, in all, about 45 minutes, gently shaking the *poêlon* from time to time. If the heat is right, the vegetables will sweat and colour in their own liquid; should they threaten to dry out, add a few drops of water.

Squeeze a few drops of lemon juice over each chicory head, spoon a bit of cream over each, cover again and leave over low heat for a few seconds or a minute – only until the cream has mostly melted down and mingled with the caramelised juices in the bottom of the *poêlon*.

OXTAIL AND PIG'S EAR STEW

INGREDIENTS
METRIC AND IMPERIAL

1 large or 2 smaller oxtails, cut into sections weighing about 1.8–2.3 kg (4–5 lb) in total

1 celery stick

section of leek or leek greens

2.5 cm (1 in) thick slice green (unsmoked) bacon, cut crosswise into about 12 wedges

about 3 tbsp olive oil

225 g (8 oz) onions, chopped

225 g (8 oz) carrots, cut into pieces

salt

2 pig's ears

large pinch of sugar

about 4 tbsp flour

additional wine or stock or water

FOR THE MARINADE

about 1 tbsp olive oil

1 onion, thinly sliced

1–2 carrots, thinly sliced

3–4 garlic cloves, crushed beneath a knife blade

large pinch of mixed dried herbs

branches of thyme and parsley (or parsley root)

2 bay leaves

1 bottle of Cahors or other good, rustic, young, deeply coloured red wine

FOR THE GARNISH

about 2 heads (24–30 cloves) fresh, unsprouted garlic, peeled

450 g (1 lb) small firm-fleshed potatoes

finely chopped fresh parsley (page 15)

Serves 4

Except for variations in garnish and the presence of the pig's ears, this is a very basic stew type: boeuf à la Bourguignonne, coq-au-vin and matelote of veal are all essentially the same recipe, and pork, lamb, rabbit, wild boar and venison stews can be prepared in the same way. From the larger animals, gelatinous cuts – shanks or neck – are the best and the cheapest. Civets of hare or rabbit (wild or hutch) are the same except that the sauce is thickened with the animal's blood at the last minute: the blood is added off the heat and the pan returned to very low heat, swirled and gently stirred until the red colour of the blood gives way to the deep hue of bitter chocolate, but the sauce must not return to a boil lest it break, losing its velvety texture and becoming granular.

Cooking times vary and low simmers are essential. Pork and veal require no more than half the cooking time of the following recipe; a tender rabbit needs no more than 40 minutes. The only dependable rule is to cook until tender but still intact. Garnishes are always added 15 to 30 minutes before serving to ensure the retention of individual shapes, textures and flavours. The lardons and garlic cloves that garnish the following preparation are good with any of these stews. A traditional Burgundian garnish is composed of lardons, little glazed onions and mushrooms, either rapidly sautéed or brought to a boil with a bit of water, a squeeze of lemon and a dab of butter. Pre-cooked chestnuts often garnish pork stews. Except when a very dark sauce is basic to the character of a dish, white wine may be substituted for red – or you can gather together bottle ends of white, rosé and red ...

Any leftover, degreased, jellied roasting juices of poultry, veal or pork are a valuable addition and, if stock is on hand, a cupful or so may supplement the wine. To many stews the stock brings not only flavour but a precious gelatinous body; the following preparation draws sufficient body from the ears.

The garlic cloves, despite their abundance, are suave and unaggressive. The ears are melting and succulent.

Cut the oxtail into sections and remove superficial fat. In a large bowl, toss the pieces of oxtail with the spoonful of olive oil and dry ingredients of the marinade. Pour over enough wine to immerse the meat completely (page 16) and marinate, covered, for several hours or, refrigerated, overnight.

Remove the oxtail to a colander to drain thoroughly, collecting the liquid. Remove the herb branches and the bay leaves, enclose them in the celery, split the leek and tie up into a bouquet garni. Dry the pieces of oxtail in a towel or paper towels.

In a large, heavy sauté pan, cook the bacon wedges in the olive oil over low heat until lightly coloured. Add the cut-up onions and carrots and a little salt, and continue to cook over low heat, stirring regularly, for about 30 minutes or until the vegetables are lightly coloured and softened.

Meanwhile, put the pig's ears in a large saucepan, cover with cold water and bring slowly to the boil. Drain and rinse in cold water. Set aside.

Empty completely the contents of the sauté pan into a sieve placed over a bowl to collect the fat. Pick out the bacon and put aside.

Pour the drained oil back into the sauté pan, adding more olive oil if necessary to coat the bottom of the pan. Over medium heat, brown the pieces of oxtail, salted, on all sides (they should fit the pan without being packed). Sprinkle with sugar and turn the meat over in the pan to caramelise. Sprinkle with the flour and turn the meat two or three times more for two minutes until the flour has lightly browned. Return the carrots and onions to the pan and pour over part or all of the marinade. Scrape with a wooden spoon to dislodge and dissolve caramelised material and remove from the heat.

Arrange the pig's ears and the pieces of oxtail in an earthenware *daubière*, preferably, or a *pot-au-feu* – or a large, heavy, enamelled ironware casserole – so that no space is wasted. Pour over the contents of the sauté pan, wash it out with a little more wine, stock or water and pour that over, then add enough additional liquid to immerse the meats and vegetables.

Whether using earthenware or a metal casserole, you will probably need an asbestos pad or other heat disperser to maintain a bare simmer with only a whisper of movement at the stew's surface. Cover, bring to the boiling point and adjust the heat accordingly; cook, undisturbed, for about 3½ hours.

Remove the pieces of oxtail and pig's ears, one by one, to a platter. Squeeze the bouquet garni to extract the juices and discard it. Pour the contents of the *daubière* into a sieve over a bowl, pressing to extract the juices; discard the pressed vegetables. Slice the pig's ears, lengthwise, into strips. Replace the sections of oxtail in the *daubière*, place the fragile strips of pig's ears loosely on top and scatter over the reserved bacon wedges. Hold, covered, while finishing the sauce.

Parboil the garlic cloves at a simmer in salted water until just tender but not mushy – about 12 minutes. Drain.

Skim as much fat as possible from the surface of the strained cooking liquid, then pour the liquid into a saucepan. Bring it to the boil, lower the heat and move the saucepan half off the heat so that a light boil is maintained on one side of the surface while the other side remains still. A skin will form on the still side and should be gently pulled to the edge with a tablespoon. When the sauce is completely cleansed (20 to 30 minutes), taste for salt and pour the sauce back over the meats in the *daubière*. Replace it, covered, over low heat until ready to serve, adding the precooked garlic cloves about 10 minutes before serving and laying the potatoes, first boiled in their skins and peeled while hot, atop.

Remove the meats, garnish and sauce to a heated platter or earthenware gratin dish. Spinkle with parsley before serving.

Oxtail and Pig's Ear Stew

HONEY-GLAZED APPLE TART

INGREDIENTS
METRIC AND IMPERIAL

about 450 g (1 lb) puff pastry (page 21)

1 egg yolk, beaten with a few drops of water

3–4 apples

melted unsalted butter

sugar

about 2 tbsp honey

Serves 4

I prefer to use russet or reinette apples for all apple desserts. Use what you can find, bearing in mind that very tart apples are not the best for these purposes.

Use very cold pastry, lightly floured, on a lightly floured slab of marble or board. First tap the pastry a few times with the side of the rolling pin to flatten it slightly and render it more supple. Roll it into a long rectangle, wide enough and long enough to cut borders from the trimmings. Cut out a neat rectangle and remove it to a baking tray. With a pastry brush, paint egg yolk over the surface.

Cut borders 1–2 cm (½–⅔ in) wide from the trimmings, lay them in place and paint the surfaces with egg yolk. Prick the bottom of the pastry case, inside the borders, repeatedly, in rows, with the tines of a fork and, with the fork overturned, drag a criss–cross pattern lightly on to the borders. If space permits, refrigerate the baking tray while preparing the apples.

Preheat the oven to 230°C (450°F or Mark 8).

Split each apple vertically, remove the core and peel it, then slice the apples crosswise (in the opposite sense of the split).

Lay the apple slices in the pastry case, overlapping them, in one or two rows, depending on the width of the pastry. Paint the surface of the apples with melted butter and sprinkle over sugar. Bake for 5 minutes, then turn the oven down to 180°C (350°F or Mark 4) and continue baking for about 40 minutes or until the pastry borders are risen, rich golden and crisp.

Warm the honey in a bowl immersed in hot water. If necessary, add a few drops of hot water to the honey to render it more fluid. Paint the surface of the apples with honey after removing from the oven.

It is often difficult to find the right serving dish for this shape of pastry; we used a board covered with foil for the photo.

Opposite: Honey-Glazed Apple Tart

Southern Bordeaux

The region of Graves, whose name derives from its coarse, gravelly soil, stretches approximately 50 km (30 miles) south from the city of Bordeaux to Langon, along the left bank of the Garonne river; Sauternes forms a small enclave within its southern tip. The Médoc, to the north of Bordeaux, is a geological and geographical continuation of Graves: both are punctuated by the arid mounds of Pyrenean pebble deposits, or *croupes*, on which are planted the most famous vineyards of the Bordelais; both share the same general microclimate, protected from ocean winds by the forest of the Landes, while the proximity both of the Atlantic and of the Garonne and Gironde rivers discourages extremes of seasonal temperatures.

Were it not for the white wines of Graves and Sauternes, this chapter would have been incorporated into the following chapter, for the red wines of Graves are of the same family as those of the Médoc and, on occasion, tasted blindly, it is possible to mistake one for the other. The Cabernet-Sauvignon grape dominates in their make-up, in combination with Merlot and a lesser quantity of Cabernet franc; Malbec is progressively disappearing from the vineyards. These red wines are commonly described as having a more earthy taste than the Médocs; cigar boxes, cedar and smokiness are sometimes evoked. Less specifically, a certain restraint or austerity, often disguised by a rich fruit when still in the wood, and a marked capacity for evolution in depth and a widening spectrum of nuance with the passage of time, are typical. These qualities seem to me to be best thrown into relief by the uncomplicated flavours of roast or grilled meats.

Fifteen Graves growths, all from the northern part of the region (listed alphabetically – except for Château

VEAL SWEETBREADS SERVED WITH A SAUTERNES

Apéritif: Champagne

Oysters and Green Sausages
DOMAINE DE CHEVALIER BLANC
1983

Veal Sweetbreads Sweated in Sauternes
CHATEAU FILHOT 1970

Leg of Lamb on a Bed of Potatoes, Green Beans
CHATEAU HAUT-BAILLY 1975

Cheeses
MALARTIC-LAGRAVIERES
*(or Domaine de Chevalier, La Mission
Haut-Brion, Haut-Brion, etc. 1971, 1970, 1966,
or older)*

Almond Bavarian Cream and Peaches in Sauternes
CHATEAU DOISY-DUBROCA 1920

Haut-Brion, which heads the list – with no indication of varying levels of quality), were officially recognised in 1959 as classified growths. Pessac (Haut-Brion, Pape-Clément) and Talence (La Mission-, Latour- and Laville-Haut-Brion) are in the suburbs of Bordeaux; Domaine de Chevalier, Haut-Bailly, Malartic-Lagravière, Carbonnieux, Fieuzal and Olivier are all in Léognan, 15 km (9 miles) south of Bordeaux; Bouscaut is in Cadaujac; La Tour-Martillac and Smith-Haut-Lafitte in Martillac; Couhins in Villenave d'Ornon – none are far distant.

The two principal white grape varieties are Sauvignon and Sémillon, the first admired for the immediacy and freshness of its fruit, the second for its lasting power and the eloquence of its bouquet after the first flush of youth has passed. The most distinguished white growths in Graves are each very different in style from the others. The magic of the soil contributes to these differences, along with the proportional relationship of the grape varieties and differences in fermenting and raising techniques. Malartic-Lagravière is all Sauvignon, but very untypical and this must be attributed to the soil. Sauvignon dominates at Domaine de Chevalier and Carbonnieux, Sémillon dominates at Laville-Haut-Brion, Bouscaut and Haut-Brion have equal quantities of each. Haut-Brion, Malartic-Lagravière and Carbonnieux ferment in stainless steel tanks, the others in barrels. Haut-Brion raises the wine for a year in all new oak before bottling; Domaine de Chevalier for 18 months in part new oak; the others for six months, often with brief passages in new oak, a question of seasoning. Carbonnieux and Malartic-Lagravière can be drunk younger than the others, which usually show best after eight or ten years. All age well and some gain in nuance and complexity for 40 or 50 years while retaining an astonishing freshness.

The wines of Sauternes, made predominantly from Sémillon with about 20% Sauvignon and, sometimes, a bit of Muscadelle, owe their existence to a very special microclimate, created by the conjunction of the little Ciron river with the Garonne. It is responsible for the autumnal morning mists which, followed by sunny days, encourage the healthy proliferation of noble rot, or *Botrytis cinerea*, a fungus which withers the grapes, concentrating the grape sugars and altering their chemical structure as well, to produce exotic flavours unknown to wines made from normally ripened grapes. Botrytis spreads irregularly, both on the bunches of grapes and amongst the vines, imposing repeated passages through the vineyards when picking to select only the botrytis-altered grapes from each bunch. Some vineyards limit these passages to three, picking whole bunches of grapes when possible, others to four or five. A few will go all the way. At Château d'Yquem, there may be up to a dozen passages in a difficult year, stretched over two months or more; the picking may last five times as long as that of a great growth of red or dry white wine to produce one-fifth of the quantity. Vinification methods vary from temperature-controlled fermentations in stainless steel tanks, in which the wine may also be stored until bottling, to the completely traditional vinification at Yquem, where the wine is fermented in new oak barrels and is raised in the same barrels for three and a half years before bottling.

The official 1855 classification of the white wines of the Gironde, all limited to Sauternes, lists Yquem as Superior First Growth (1er Cru Supérieur), followed by nine first growths and eleven second growths. Now, as then, no one disputes Yquem's supremacy. Others have slipped or improved, one no longer exists and several unclassed growths are the equals of second or first growths. The most distressing slip is that of Rayne-Vigneau, which made sublime wines in the past and, in a rational world, should be second only to Yquem, but its proprietors have opted for maximum production, limited botrytis and subsequent chaptalisation; the wines are not unpleasant but they are distinctly thin and lacking in dimension.

Five villages – Sauternes, Fargues, Bommes, Preignac and Barsac – are included in the Sauternes *appellation contrôlée*. For a reason that no one can explain, Barsac was given its appellation apart, while retaining the right to call itself Sauternes, a privilege the other villages felt was being abused; recent legislation permits the growers of Barsac to choose between the appellations Sauternes and Barsac, but they are no longer permitted to use both on their labels. Some of the better classified growths from Barsac are Climens, Coutet, Nairac, Doisy-Daëne and Broustet; from the other villages, Suduiraut, Rieussec, Sigalas-Rabaud and Filhot. A tiny fraction of the Château de Fargues estate, property of the Lur Saluces family since 1472, has been planted to vines in the last century. The wine is splendid, as is that of Raymond-

Lafon, also unclassified, which is owned by Pierre Meslier, estate manager of both Yquem and Fargues.

The lifespan of traditionally made Sauternes is long. One can only guess at the lifespan of Yquem for the oldest known bottles are still in perfect condition. Recently, at a marathon dinner-wine-tasting organised at Château d'Yquem by the German wine collector, Hardy Rodenstock (14 hours at table, four services punctuated by Champagne breaks, a dozen courses and 62 wines), four ancient Yquems wound up the first service; 1858, 1847 (the most celebrated nineteenth-century vintage of Yquem), 1811 (the famous comet year), and (circa) 1750 (rescued apparently from the cellars of the Russian czars). All were luscious, liquorous and in harmonious balance. The 1858, 1811 and 1750 resembled one another. The 1847 was simply the most astonishing wine I have ever tasted. An attempt at description is useless except to note that the aura of bitter chocolate, common to certain very old Yquems, was present. It was easy, at that moment, to understand why, at the turn of the century, Yquem 1847 was so often placed on menus destined to honour crowned heads.

The incorporation of a Sauternes into the main body of a menu intimidates many people who prefer to think of it as a dessert wine. This was not always so. Throughout the nineteenth century and until the First World War, Sauternes was the wine most often served with fish on menus for special occasions. In fact, the sweetness of these wines, tempered by a refreshing acidity, a delicate veil of bitterness, a voluptuous texture and an abundance of taste and scent associations, raises no barrier to their alliance with any number of savoury foods. In the Bordelais, Sauternes is the automatic accompaniment to foie gras and to Roquefort or other blue cheeses. While writing *Yquem* (to celebrate the bicentenary of the Lur Saluces family's presence there), I experimented with a number of dishes for the chapter entitled Yquem and the Table. Amongst those which I thought to be especially successful (with an Yquem 1976) was the sweetbread preparation; its predilection for Sauternes was reconfirmed after photographing it for this book when we drank the Filhot 1970 with it.

The following menu is, in part, a souvenir of Sunday lunches shared at Domaine de Chevalier with Claude and Monik Ricard and their family, oysters and leg of lamb being classic elements in those meals. Claude delights in creating instructive (and humbling) tasting games. Once, with the cheeses, we were asked to guess the vintages of two old wines from the *domaine*, one tawnier and obviously older than the other. I guessed the younger wine to be 1928, probably with a Malartic-Lagravière 1928, drunk the previous day with the Marly family, uppermost in my mind, floundered a bit and guessed the older to be 1926. Both were 1928. Another time we were told that our glasses would contain four 1967s – Domaine de Chevalier, Haut-Brion, Latour and Lafite – but not in what order. Most of us sorted them out, but the similarity in structure and taste of the Domaine de Chevalier to the Latour gave pause for thought.

TIMING

The green sausages (except for grilling), the Bavarian cream and the peaches in Sauternes are prepared in advance; the sweetbreads are pre-prepared for braising and the leg of lamb is prepared for roasting in advance. The mirepoix may be prepared in advance or you can as easily put it to work an hour before the meal. Open the oysters at the same time, then prepare the potatoes and, half an hour before going to table, put them in the oven and put the sweetbreads to sweat. Add the leg of lamb to the potatoes 15 minutes later, remembering that, when cooked, it may be held in a tepid oven for a while with no inconvenience. Begin grilling the sausages when the lamb goes in.

OYSTERS AND GREEN SAUSAGES

INGREDIENTS
METRIC AND IMPERIAL

6 oysters per person

lemon halves or sections, to accompany the oysters

FOR THE SAUSAGES

700 g (1½ lb) fresh spinach, stalks removed

700 g (1½ lb) basic sausage meat (page 19)

persillade (page 15)

caul, soaked in tepid water if salted or frozen

Serves 4

Freshly opened oysters and hot, grilled sausages, either chipolata or crépinettes, accompanied by a white Graves, is a typically Bordelais concept. The addition of spinach to the sausage meat is not traditional but its natural affinity to things of the sea makes it logical. The alternating bites of hot and cold, moistened by the slightly metallic overtones of the Graves, play together very nicely.

The inspiration for the spinach crépinettes is drawn from the caillettes of the Vaucluse in the region around Avignon, in which a chopped mixture of pork innards and salt pork replaces the sausage meat used here. They are sometimes served hot but, more often, cold as a starter. In another context, these sausages are also good eaten cold.

If you can arrange to have the oysters opened by a professional within the hour preceding the meal, do so. Otherwise, you will need a short, stiff-bladed oyster knife; hold the oyster in a folded towel, flat side facing up, and force the tip of the knife between the two shells at the join; when the muscle relaxes, slide the knife blade against the inside upper surface (of the flat shell) to sever the oyster's attachment to the shell. Try to lose as little as possible of the liquid contained in the deep shell. Discard the flat shells.

To make the sausages, first wash the spinach in several waters, then parboil in abundant boiling salted water for less than a minute. Drain, refresh under cold running water and squeeze dry. The spinach, when squeezed, forms a firm ball. To chop it, slice the ball thinly, give the mass a quarter turn and chop finely through the slices.

Mix together the sausage meat, spinach and persillade very thoroughly. With your hands, form patties approximately 2.5–4 cm (1–1½ in) thick and 7–8 cm (3 in) in diameter. Place each on a square of caul large enough to enclose the patty easily, fold the edges up over the top and press in place to seal the patty in the caul.

Grill the sausages beneath a heat source or, if convenient, over hot coals until golden brown on both surfaces and firm to the touch, about 7 minutes on each side. Serve on separate plates at the same time as the oysters.

Opposite: Oysters and Green Sausages (crépinettes) with a white Graves

VEAL SWEETBREADS SWEATED IN SAUTERNES

INGREDIENTS
METRIC AND IMPERIAL

900 g (2 lb) veal sweetbreads

finely chopped mirepoix (page 18), based on 100 g (4 oz) each of onions and carrots

salt

about 4 tbsp Sauternes

freshly ground pepper

about 4 tbsp double cream

Serves 4

Whatever the final preparation, sweetbreads should first be soaked in cold water for several hours or overnight, with several changes of water or in an over-running basin fed by a trickling tap. Put into a large saucepan, cover abundantly with cold water and bring slowly to a near simmer. Hold over low heat, beneath the boil (80°–85°C/180°–190°F), for about 20 minutes, then drain and immerse in cold water. Surface membranes, cartilaginous tubes and clinging pieces of fat should be removed, but the fine membranes that hold the lobes of flesh together should not be torn out. The sweetbreads will lose in succulence if pre-cooked at a boiling temperature or if placed under weight after cleaning.

In a heavy saucepan or *sauteuse* of a size just to hold the sweetbreads placed side by side, arrange the sweetbreads, lightly salted, on the bed of mirepoix. Sprinkle over Sauternes to moisten the bottom of the pan, then loosely press a sheet of buttered greaseproof or parchment paper to the surface of the sweetbreads. Cover the pan tightly and cook (sweat) over very low heat for about 30 minutes. The vapours will condense on the underside of the sheet of paper, running back over the sweetbreads in a continuing basting process.

Remove and discard the paper. Grind pepper over to taste and dab the cream over the surface of the sweetbreads. Cover and leave for another minute or so or until the cream has melted and mingled with the mirepoix and the juices. Serve, directly from the *sauteuse*, on to preheated plates.

LEG OF LAMB ON A BED OF POTATOES

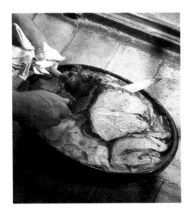

Carving the Lamb on a Bed of Potatoes

When cooking the leg of lamb – or another roast – separately from the potatoes, I often spread a layer of creamed sorrel (raw sorrel chiffonade, salted, cooked slowly in butter until melted, cream added and slightly reduced) over the potatoes' surface before putting them to bake.

Try to use a variety of potato that does not disintegrate during cooking. The texture of the gratin is most attractive when large potatoes are used, sliced as thinly as possible, lengthwise. The traditional potato-slicer, known as a mandoline, will do the job most easily. If slicing by hand, first remove a couple of slices to form a flat, steady base.

At first try, it is easy to misjudge the quantity of water required for cooking – less than enough to cover the potatoes and onions in the saucepan and just enough almost to surface when spread in the gratin dish.

Remove all surface fat from the leg of lamb. In a mortar, pound the garlic, salt, pepper and herbs to a paste. With the pestle, mix in enough white wine to turn the mixture liquid. With a small, sharply pointed knife, pierce deep vents in the lamb eight or ten in all, on the bias and pointed toward the thick end of the leg, wide enough at the entrance to receive the tip of a teaspoon. Open up each vent with your little finger and, with a teaspoon, pour some of the garlic-herb mixture into each. Any remaining mixture can be smeared around the bone and over the surface. Pour a little olive oil over the leg and rub all surfaces with your hands, leaving an all-over film of oil. If prepared so far in advance as to require refrigeration, remove the leg from the refrigerator at least an hour before roasting.

Preheat the oven to 230°C (450°F or Mark 8).

Put the potatoes, onions and a sprinkling of salt into a large saucepan. Pour over enough boiling water partially to immerse the vegetables and, over medium heat, bring to the boil, stirring and scraping the bottom of the pan with a wooden spoon to prevent sticking. Pour the contents of the pan into a buttered oval gratin dish, long enough to contain the leg of lamb, and spread out evenly, rearranging potato slices, when necessary, to form a smooth surface. Scatter a few shavings of cold butter over the surface and put into the oven.

Fifteen minutes later, place the leg of lamb on top, reserving any marinating liquid that has settled to the bottom of the dish. Fifteen minutes later, reduce the heat to 160°C (325°F or Mark 3). Fifteen minutes later, baste the leg with the reserved marinade. Fifteen or 20 minutes later, turn off the oven and leave the dish in for another 20 to 30 minutes, or until ready to serve, 1¼ to 1½ hours after first putting the potatoes to bake.

INGREDIENTS
METRIC AND IMPERIAL

1 leg of lamb, weighing about 2.7 kg (6 lb)

1–2 garlic cloves, peeled

large pinch of coarse salt

freshly ground pepper

large pinch of mixed dried herbs

white wine

olive oil

FOR THE POTATOES

900 g–1.4 kg (2–3 lb) large potatoes, peeled and thinly sliced lengthwise

450 g (1 lb) onions, halved and thinly sliced

salt

25–40 g (1–1½ oz) unsalted butter

Serves 4

GREEN BEANS

Good beans can take from two to ten minutes to cook, depending on the variety and the stage of development; those that require the least amount of time are the best. Any that demand much more than 10 minutes to become tender are best cooked and then sautéed in hot olive oil with a garlic persillade (page 15) and a final squeeze of lemon to disguise their banality or sautéed with onions and tomatoes.

Don't be alarmed at the quantity of salt – the beans require a large quantity of boiling water and the shorter their cooking time, the more salt is necessary to season them only delicately; nearly all the salt is discarded with the cooking water.

Put the beans in a large saucepan, throw over the salt, place over high heat and pour over an abundance of rapidly boiling water. Boil, uncovered, until barely tender, removing a bean from the water and biting into it to test. Drain and toss over high heat for a few seconds to dry them out. Off the heat, add the butter and continue to toss until it is absorbed.

INGREDIENTS
METRIC AND IMPERIAL

700 g (1½ lb) green beans, topped and tailed, rinsed and drained

large handful of coarse sea salt

25–50 g (1–2 oz) cold unsalted butter, diced

Serves 4

ALMOND BAVARIAN CREAM

AND PEACHES IN SAUTERNES

INGREDIENTS
METRIC AND IMPERIAL

FOR THE BAVARIAN CREAM

225 g (8 oz) shelled almonds, peeled (page 20)

4–5 bitter almonds, peeled (page 20)

350 ml (12 fl oz) water

350 ml (12 fl oz) milk

1½ tbsp powdered gelatine

50 g (2 oz) sugar

small pinch of salt

250 ml (8 fl oz) whipping cream

FOR THE PEACHES

450 g (1 lb) ripe, unbruised yellow peaches

about 3 tbsp sugar

Sauternes

small handful of shelled pistachios, peeled (page 20) and coarsely chopped

Serves 4

To make a traditional blanc-manger, the soupy, ground almond, water and milk mixture of the following recipe is twisted repeatedly in a strong kitchen towel and only the extracted liquid, or almond milk, is used in the preparation. This is a fast and easy version, with all the flavour but lacking the silken texture of a blanc-manger.

Almonds and peaches, separate or in combination, are perhaps two of the most successful accompanying flavours to a Sauternes. If the Bavarian cream is presented in a single, large mould, it is more practical to hold most of the peaches and pistachios in reserve to garnish the individual plates at the moment of service.

If bitter almonds are unavailable, substitute a few drops of almond essence or bitter almond essence.

Grind the almonds finely in a food processor, gradually adding two-thirds of the water and, finally, about one-third of the milk, to create a thick, soupy consistency.

Put the gelatine to soften in the remaining water. Combine the remaining milk, the sugar and salt in a saucepan and bring to the boiling point, stirring to dissolve the sugar. Remove from the heat and stir in the softened gelatine.

Whip the cream until it begins to form soft peaks – it should not be stiff. Whisk the almond mixture and the sweetened milk and gelatine mixture together in a bowl. Embed the bowl in cracked ice and stir until the gelatine begins to take. Fold in the whipped cream. Pour into individual moulds – or a single mould – that have been lightly greased with a tasteless oil, and refrigerate for several hours or overnight.

Peel the peaches and slice them into a bowl. Sprinkle the sugar over the peaches, pour over Sauternes barely to cover and refrigerate, tightly covered, for several hours.

To unmould the Bavarian creams, loosen the edges with a knife tip before dipping the bottom of each mould into hot water for a second and wiping it with a towel. The overturned mould often requires a shake to loosen the cream which clings by suction to the inside of the mould.

Present surrounded by a portion of the peach slices in their liquid and sprinkled with chopped pistachios, the remainder served apart.

Opposite: Almond Bavarian Cream and Peaches in Sauternes

Northern Bordeaux

The Médoc, Saint-Emilion and Pomerol appellations are all red wines (a few whites are made in Médoc which carry the generic Bordeaux *appellation contrôlée*). As with the Graves reds, the three principal grape varieties are Cabernet-Sauvignon, Cabernet franc and Merlot but, whereas in Médoc and Graves, Cabernet-Sauvignon dominates, the ratio is inverted in Saint-Emilion and Pomerol, with Merlot dominating and Cabernet franc assuming greater importance, often to the exclusion of Cabernet-Sauvignon.

Médoc is broken down into eight appellations: Médoc (the northern part of the peninsula, geographically known as Bas-Médoc), Haut-Médoc (within which lie all of the village appellations and all of the classified growths) and the village appellations of Saint-Estèphe, Pauillac, Saint-Julien, Margaux, Moulis and Listrac.

Most of Saint-Emilion's Premiers Grands Crus Classés (Ausone, Belair, Canon, Magdelaine, Pavie, La Gaffelière, Beauséjour) are clustered around the medieval hill-town of Saint-Emilion – to the west, the south and the south-east – on the slopes known as the Grande Côte and the Pied de Côte (foothill). The chalky, more or less sandy clay reposing on a fossilised sea-shell bed of limestone explains in part the predominance of Merlot; it has an affinity for this type of soil composition, more reminiscent of the Côte d'Or (although 100 million years or so more recent in geological origin) than of the pebbly slopes of Médoc and Graves. Beneath many of these vineyards lie former limestone quarries, ready-made cellars of ideal temperature and humidity.

The Graves de Saint-Emilion, a plateau of undulating, gravelly mounds on a bedrock of ferruginous sandstone,

Duck Terrine
(1) CHATEAU DE PEZ (SAINT-
ESTEPHE) 1978 *(or (2) Château Monbousquet
(Saint-Emilion) 1983 or (3) Clos René (Pomerol) 1981)*

Brochettes of Scallops, Monkfish and Bacon
(1) CHATEAU HAUT-BATAILLEY
(PAUILLAC) 1976 *(or (2) Château Corbin-
Michotte (Saint-Emilion Grand Cru Classé) 1982 or
(3) Château Petit-Village (Pomerol) 1981)*

Roast Pheasant, Potato Straw Cake
(1) LES FORTS DE LATOUR
(PAUILLAC) 1971 *(or (2) Château Canon
(Saint-Emilion Premier Grand Cru Classé) 1979 or
(3) Château La Conseillante (Pomerol) 1981)*

Cheeses
(1) CHATEAU COS D'ESTOURNEL
(SAINT-ESTEPHE) 1966 *(or (2) Château
Figeac (Saint-Emilion Premier Grand Cru Classé) 1975 or
(3) Château Trotanoy (Pomerol) 1975)*

Pear and Red Wine Ice

not unlike the mounds of gravel that mark the great growths of Sauternes, Graves and the Médoc, borders on Pomerol and forms part of the geological entity called the Haute Terrace of Pomerol. On the Saint-Emilion side, it is mostly shared by Châteaux Figeac and Cheval Blanc. Figeac is planted to approximately 35% with Cabernet-Sauvignon, 35% with Cabernet franc and the remainder with Merlot; Cheval Blanc counts two-thirds Cabernet franc to one of Merlot. Both Figeac and Cheval Blanc are very different from other Saint-Emilions; they are also very different from one another and, more surprisingly, very different from their neighbours in Pomerol with whom they share the terrace of gravel. Figeac inclines toward spices, nuance and exotic memories, Cheval Blanc is full and spherical; the one like fine silk, the other a sumptuous, enveloping fur.

On the Pomerol side, the terrace of gravel is dominated in altitude and prestige by Château Pétrus; in *Les Grands Vins de Saint-Emilion, Pomerol et Fronsac* (1983), Henri Enjalbert attributes the uniqueness of Pétrus (mostly Merlot with about five per cent Cabernet franc) to the structure of the 'island' upon which the vines are planted. It is a mound of decalcified and, therefore, relatively acid sandy clay surmounting sandstone bedrock and subsoils and composed in varying degrees of clay, decayed bedrock and river-bed sands. This peculiar structure, devoid of gravel at the heart of a sea of gravel, is shared in part by the neighbouring vineyards of Vieux Château Certan and l'Evangile. All of the finest growths of Pomerol crowd around, sharing the famous Haute Terrace, the others sloping off into sandier soils.

The wines of these different regions seem to me best understood and appreciated when placed in a suite with others of their own kin. For that reason, I have presented three choices of wine successions in the menu (follow the numbers on page 87: all the 1s form a suite, all the 2s form another and so on). The specific wines are only suggestions and all are replaceable on condition that one remain within the same region and progress from lighter and simpler to fuller and more complex – usually, but not necessarily, from younger to older. This can be done as well with a single growth, moving from younger and slighter through older and tougher vintages, as with younger and lesser growths through older and greater growths. The latter often perform admirably in years which receive bad notes from the vintage charts and the journalists. A different formula has been adapted to the Pomerols, beginning with a lighter style, followed by a couple of classics, all of the same vintage, and finishing with an older vintage of a denser style.

Bordeaux is a bundle of souvenirs, above all the 1961 vintage. It was then with my brother James that I met the trio of close friends who lured me, by gentle coercion, into a writing career of which I had never dreamt: Madeleine Decure, editor of *Cuisine et Vins de France*, Odette Kahn, her assistant, who became editor at Madeleine's death, and Michel Lemonnier. Odette has followed Madeleine; *Cuisine et Vins de France* is now in glossy, commercial hands; Michel is in fine form.

Our first lunch that year, with the magazine's 'Amitiés Gastronomiques Internationales' – in later years to be replaced by early morning tastings accompanied by entrecôtes, grilled out-of-doors over the embers of vine prunings, and chopped shallots tossed in long-handled frying pans over the same embers – was on the shaded lawn at Haut-Brion. At Yquem, the old cellar master, Roger Bureau, long since retired, whose grand moustaches and benevolent mien have been reproduced in endless wine books, received us to taste the young 1955. Everyone was serving '55 that year.

At Château Latour, before the property changed hands and the installations were modernised, the men passed the grapes by hand through wooden grills to remove the stems before throwing them into the fermenting vats.

In Saint-Emilion, at Château Grand-Mayne, we tasted at its inception the 1961, a rough mouthful thrown into perspective a couple of hours later, at lunch, by the Grand-Mayne 1955, a firm, handsome wine with a rustic cast, a loyal reflection of its maker, the late Jean Nony, whose son, Jean-Pierre, is now master at Grand-Mayne. In Pomerol, Madame Loubat served us Pétrus 1955 and the afternoon wound up with the Clauzel family in the park at Beauregard to the accompaniment of another 1955, a couple of cases of which, thanks to my brother, found their way to my cellar in the weeks to follow.

In Saint Emilion at Château Monbousquet I remember drinking the half-fermented must, and no one could forget Daniel Querre, bigger than life, his thunderous, resounding voice tempered by a fine sense of theatre, and his love for check caps, rustic food and the hearty, chewy fruit of a young Monbousquet. Now, Alain, who has inherited his father's open, generous bonhomie, and

Sheila are the ones who receive at Monbousquet.

Above all, perhaps, a vignette of an old-fashioned couple remains etched in my mind's eye as a symbol of that trip: Thierry Manoncourt's father and mother, with radiant smiles and erect dignity, waving good-bye from the threshold of Château Figeac. Today Thierry and Marie-France wave from the same threshold with the same warmth.

The Loudenne blanc apéritif of this menu is in memory of Martin Bamford, whose glorious reign at Château Loudenne (Médoc) was cut short during the vintage of 1982 – his vintage was 1941. Like nearly everyone who has written something about wine, I have delicious memories of Martin's extraordinarily civilised table and hospitality, of Sylvain, the most attentive butler in the world, and of the remarkable meals produced by Sylvain's wife, Josette, under Martin's watchful eye; of meals shared with Francis Fouquet, Loudenne's oenologist and administrator, and with Robert and Edith Dousson, proprietors of Château de Pez; of Sunday evenings, on Sylvain's and Josette's day off, the week's international guests having departed, spent fiddling around in the kitchen preparing meals for Martin's Médocain friends. Jean-Michel Cazes, proprietor of Lynch-Bages, has since reminded me of one of those productions, crowned by a leg of milk lamb masked in a high, red and purple striped dome of aubergine and tomato fans, surrounded with aromatic vegetables sprinkled with Loudenne blanc and olive oil and baked beneath foil to succulence.

The seafood and bacon brochettes and the Haut-Batailley 1976 are a souvenir of a lunch at Château Ducru-Beaucaillou (Saint-Julien) with Jean-Eugène and Monique Borie. The alliance was surprising and perfect. Grilled steaks and ceps were accompanied by a Ducru-Beaucaillou 1966 and the cheeses by a Ducru-Beaucaillou 1953, both of lean elegance and high breeding, the '66 having just flowered into maturity, the '53 an ethereal and multi-faceted wine of the spirit, the kind that lives and evolves in memory.

For reasons of discretion, I have recommended no very old wines, but I do not understand the disdain, professed by some oenologists and writers, for old wine. My cellar contains a diminishing stock of Rausan-Ségla and Léoville-Poyferré, 1899 and 1900, from the cellars of the Lawton family (Bordeaux wine brokers since 1742), which have never failed to astonish more practised palates than my own. Wonderful meals with Robert and Ninette Place, then proprietors of Château Bouscaut, tasting trips back through the fifties, forties and thirties, always winding up with a 1929, a 1928 or a 1926, are forever stamped in my memory, as is a lunch for six, organised some 15 years ago at Mouton-Rothschild by Philippe Cottin, Baron Philippe's administrator.

The following wines were drunk: Mouton-Baron-Philippe (now Mouton-Baronne-Philippe) 1961, Pichon-Longueville (Baron) 1929, Latour 1926, Margaux 1924, La Lagune 1900, Mouton-Rothschild 1899, Mouton-Rothschild 1895, Mouton-Rothschild 1878, Yquem 1921. The bottles had been stood upright three days earlier, uncorked four hours earlier and decanted an hour before lunch. The Mouton-Baron-Philippe was a good, solid Pauillac; the Pichon was a bit bizarre with a delicate scent that gave no warning of the flavours of ginger and burnt, overcooked jam; the Mouton 1895 was slipping and would probably have been in fine shape had it been decanted just before serving.

The others were astounding wines: the Latour a slumbering, primordial giant whose wild fruit and vigour began to swell only an hour after being poured, the Margaux a joyous and intricate chamber music, and the 1899 Mouton still a bit jealous of its majesty. The Mouton 1878 can only be likened to the Parthenon, but the heart-breaker was La Lagune 1900, a serene and fragile lacework of distant memories and suffused harmony, with no thread broken.... Yquem 1921 was Yquem 1921; there is nothing else like it.

TIMING

The terrine is prepared days ahead, the ice can be prepared the previous day, the fish and bacon can be skewered and marinated, ready for grilling, an hour or so in advance and the pheasant trussed and barded in advance; the potatoes can be grated, rinsed, drained and rolled up tightly in a towel just before going to table.

Put the brochettes to grill only when guests are nearly finished with the terrine. Put the potatoes to cook just before serving the brochettes and put the pheasant in the oven after the brochettes are served.

DUCK TERRINE

INGREDIENTS
METRIC AND IMPERIAL

3 or 4 ducks, with giblets

100 g (4 oz) poultry livers

3 garlic cloves, pounded to a paste with a pinch of coarse salt

3 large handfuls of semi-fresh breadcrumbs without crusts

stock (page 18), made from the chopped duck carcasses, necks and wingtips, strained, cleansed and reduced to a light glaze

225 g (8 oz) fresh pork back fat, chilled

100 g (4 oz) prosciutto, finely chopped by hand

225 g (8 oz) lean boneless veal, puréed in a food processor

450 g (1 lb) basic sausage meat (page 19)

1 large onion, finely chopped

unsalted butter for frying

75–100 g (3–4 oz), or more, black truffles, preferably fresh

75–100 g (3–4 oz) shelled pistachios, peeled (page 20) and coarsely chopped

1 tbsp dried mixed herbs

salt and freshly ground pepper

freshly ground allspice

wine such as dry white, Sauternes, Madeira or port, depending on taste

about 125 ml (4 fl oz) Cognac

4 eggs

thin sheets (bardes) of fresh pork back fat

melted lard

Serves 40 to 50

This recipe will make large terrines that will serve 40 to 50 people. The quantities may be altered to taste or cut in half, but it is impractical to make terrines of this sort in small quantities. These terrines improve, in any case, from ripening for several days before serving and, if sealed with melted lard, may be easily kept, refrigerated, for two or three weeks; deep-freezing, on the other hand, tends to alter the firm, moist compactness, the texture becoming crumbly and the meats drier, with a certain amount of liquid escaping.

Wild ducks or domesticated mallards will give a richer flavour than other domestic ducks; pheasant, partridge, woodcock, rabbit or hare may be substituted or used in combinations to create a panoply of different flavours. If woodcock is used, its innards, except for the gizzard, are pureed and added; the blood of a hare, which collects behind a membrane in the chest cavity, should be carefully poured off, when the animal is cleaned, into a bowl containing a bit of vinegar to prevent its coagulating, and added to the terrine mixture, replacing the eggs as a binder. If cleaning any of these animals yourself, care should be taken to remove the gall bladder without damaging it and discard it.

Instead of dicing the tender flesh, pork back fat and truffles, they can be cut into strips and sticks, marinated separately from the forcemeat, and assembled with alternating layers of forcemeat in the terrine, to create a more formal, decorative mosaic in cross-section.

Without truffles, the terrines will still be good but a dimension is lost. If eliminating truffles, it is a good idea to add a handful of dried morels or gyromitres (wild mushrooms), soaked, stem-ends trimmed, split, rinsed, chopped and butter-stewed.

The skin of the ducks is not used in the terrines but, rather than discard it, it can be rendered into cracklings: rub with dried herbs, salt overnight, wipe dry and cut into pieces, then cook over low heat with, to start, a few spoonfuls of water which, after evaporation, will leave the pieces of skin cooking in their own fat until crisp. These are amusing to nibble at with aperitifs or can be incorporated into an omelette.

Remove the meat from the bones and the skin. Cut the tender parts (the breasts and non-tendonous muscles from the thighs) into approximately 1 cm (½ in) dice. Scrape tendons and nervous tissue from the remaining meat, then purée it in a food processor.

Slice the fleshy lobes of the ducks' gizzards free from the tough skin; puree the gizzard lobes, hearts, livers and the poultry livers in a food processor. Combine with the puréed and diced duck meat.

Mix together the garlic and breadcrumbs and moisten with the stock. Cut the pork back fat into approximately 5 mm (¼ in) dice and add to the garlic mixture, then add the duck meat, prosciutto, veal and sausage meat.

Stew the onion gently in butter until soft but uncoloured. Peel the truffles and cut into 5 mm (¼ in) dice; finely chop the peelings and trimmings. Add the truffles and onion to the duck mixture with the pistachios, herbs, and salt, pepper and allspice to taste. Mix thoroughly with your hands. Pack the mixture into a bowl, smoothing the surface, sprinkle over wine and refrigerate, tightly covered, overnight to permit the flavours to intermingle.

Preheat the oven to 160°–180°C (325°–350°F or Mark 3–4).

Mix the Cognac and the eggs into the duck mixture, thoroughly, with your hands. The mixture should be quite loose without being pourable – add another egg and a dash of wine, if necessary. Pack it into terrines lined with bardes of pork fat. Tap the bottom of each terrine against a folded towel placed on a work surface to settle the contents and to make certain that no air pockets are trapped in the mixture. Press a barde to the surface of each, cover with a lid or a sheet of foil and cook in a *bain-marie* of hot, but not boiling, water, in the oven. A 1 litre (2 pint) terrine requires from 1 hour to 1 hour and 10 minutes, larger terrines up to 2 hours. They are ready when the juices flow clear, or when the tip of a trussing needle, thrust to the heart of the terrine, is quite warm to the touch.

Cool the terrines under weight: place a sheet of foil on the surface, then add a board or stiff piece of cardboard cut to the inside dimensions of the terrine topped with the weight. A 900 g (2 lb) weight is about right – too heavy a weight will force out too many juices and the terrine will be dry; too little weight will fail to render it sufficiently compact for easy slicing and serving. Place the terrines first on a tray as they often overflow under weight. When cooled, cover and refrigerate. For those terrines destined to be kept for more than a few days, pour melted lard over the surfaces to seal them before refrigerating.

At the moment of serving, the barde wrapping may be removed from the slices, if desired. The first slice is always difficult to remove and usually damaged; take care to use a sharp, pointed knife for slicing and to cut thoroughly through the bardes; remove the slices with the help of a spatula.

BROCHETTES OF SCALLOPS, MONKFISH AND BACON

INGREDIENTS
METRIC AND IMPERIAL

12 scallops

*about 275 g (10 oz) monkfish
fillet, cut into pieces of
approximately equal size*

3 bacon rashers, cut into squares

FOR THE MARINADE

olive oil

chopped wild fennel leaves

salt and freshly ground pepper

Serves 4

*Opposite: Brochettes of Scallops,
Monkfish and Bacon with a
Pauillac wine from the Médoc*

In wine regions where little or no white wine is made, vignerons prefer to ignore the rules that forbid the marriage of red wines with seafood and are none the worse off for that. In May and June, when shad is fished from the Gironde, it appears, grilled, at all tables, as often as not accompanied by a red wine. It is also at this season that elvers (*pibales* or *civelles*), translucent, thread-like baby eels, wrap themselves by the millions into balls and roll across the ocean floor, from their birthplace in the Sargasso sea, and up the mouths of certain rivers, of which the Gironde is one; warmed in olive oil, until opaque and white, with a couple each of bruised garlic cloves and tiny hot red peppers, elvers are a great delicacy, equally well accompanied by a firm white wine or a relatively young, cool red wine without excessive tannins.

The choice of seafood for brochettes depends mostly on the firmness of the flesh and the adaptability of its form to being cut into cubes of similar size. Salmon lends itself well and its pronounced and personal flavour is very much at home with a red wine – dill goes well with salmon but, perhaps, less well with red wine. Large prawns or shrimp are a possibility. If another herb is preferred to the fresh fennel, crumbled, dried oregano flowers are a good choice for a very different effect. Disposable bamboo skewers 30 cm (12 in) long are practical.

Toss all of the ingredients together and leave to marinate for from 15 minutes to 1 hour. Alternate the scallops and pieces of monkfish on the skewers with a square of bacon between each and grill for 10 to 12 minutes, or until the fish is opaque and firm to the touch. If grilling on a tray beneath a heat source with heat from beneath also, they need not be turned. Over embers, the most practical method is to enclose them in a double-faced grill that is turned after 5 minutes or so.

ROAST PHEASANT

INGREDIENTS
METRIC AND IMPERIAL

1 pheasant

softened unsalted butter or olive oil

salt

sheet of fresh pork back fat (barde)

Serves 4

For roasting, a pheasant should be young; hens are tenderer than cocks. Indications of youth are smooth, non-scaly feet, a supple, pliable breastbone and pointed, rather than rounded, tips to the long wing feathers. Unless a pheasant has received shot in the abdomen (in which case, it is wiser to pluck it and clean it immediately), the flesh will become more tender and flavourful with three or four days' hanging in a cool, dry, well-ventilated place (or refrigerated, unwrapped, in its feathers) before plucking. The presence of blood in the flesh of a game bird is part of its quality; if a domestic pheasant is sacrificed, it should be strangled, rather than beheaded, and not bled (this is true of guinea fowl and pigeons also). Plucking is a tiresome chore; care should be taken, particularly with the breast where the skin is most susceptible to tearing, to pinch the base of the feathers between thumb and forefinger before pulling them out with the other hand.

After plucking and singeing, if the feet are cut off 2.5 cm (1 in) or so beneath the heel, rather than at the joint, the skin and flesh of the drumstick will not pull away from the bone while cooking and the presentation will be more attractive. Trussing is easier and the result neater if the wingtips are cut off at the elbow joint, leaving only the shoulder joint attached to the body. To remove the neck, slit the neck skin the length of the back side, pull it free of the neck, cut through the neck from the back where it joins the backbone and twist it off. Pull the trachea and the oesophagus free from the neck skin before emptying the bird. The breast can only be carved neatly if the wishbone is removed before trussing: force the neck skin down to bare the upper part of the breast until the contours of the wishbone are visible. With the sharp point of a small knife, slit the flesh shallowly along the contours and against the bone, freeing the apex at the breastbone and freeing the flesh from the bone with fingertips, then pull it back from the breastbone to snap it free where it joins the wing joints.

To truss, use two 40–50 cm (15–20 in) lengths of string. Fold the neck skin flap over the back and pull the legs into place, bending the joint to place them high up against the side of the body, then run the trussing needle through the upper part of the wing joints, the neck skin and the back, pinning the skin to the back. Pierce the legs and the body high on the drumstick, near the joint, pull the string ends tightly, tie and clip the excess. Repeat with the other length of string, piercing the lower ends of the wing sections and the back and the lower ends of the drumsticks and the body. Rub the bird all over, either with a little softened butter or with olive oil, and sprinkle with salt.

A barde, or sheet of fresh pork back fat, will prevent the breast from overcooking and drying out. To bard the bird, use a sheet of fat approximately 12 × 15 cm (5 × 6 in). Place it over the breast and tie it in place with two lengths of string, encircling the bird high and low on the breast.

Preheat the oven to 230–240°C (450–475°F or Mark 8–9).

Place the bird on its back in a small heavy gratin dish or frying pan and roast for 20 minutes. Clip the barding strings and remove the barde. Clip the trussing strings and pull at the knots to remove them. With a sharp knife, slit the skin attaching the legs to the body, all the way from the back to the extremity of the abdomen, and bend the legs outward, away from the body, until the thigh and pelvic joints snap and the legs lie out from the body without resistance (this hastens the cooking of the legs which, otherwise, require a longer cooking time than the breast). Return to the hot oven for another 6 or 7 minutes. Remove to a heated platter and carve at table.

Often slices of crustless bread, crisped in butter and spread with a farce gratin, accompany roast pheasant, slices of breast placed atop when served out. To prepare a farce gratin, cook a couple of finely chopped shallots in butter until soft, add the pheasant's liver and one or two chicken livers, plus salt and pepper, and sauté for a few seconds until the surfaces are greyed. Flame with a dash of Cognac and pass through a sieve.

Roast Pheasant with a Pauillac wine from the Médoc

POTATO STRAW CAKE

INGREDIENTS
METRIC AND IMPERIAL

700 g (1½ lb) potatoes, peeled

125 g (4 oz) unsalted butter

salt and freshly ground pepper

Serves 4

Shred the potatoes to spaghetti through the medium blade of a mouli-julienne or food processor. Rinse in a basin of water, drain and roll tightly in a kitchen towel to dry.

Melt half the butter in a heavy frying pan over low to medium heat. Pack in the potatoes, smoothing the surface and edges carefully with the back of a fork, and season the surface. Place strips of butter all around the edges and cook, covered with a flat lid, for about 20 minutes or until the edges are golden and have begun to shrink from the sides of the pan (when removing the lid, lift it up and away from the pan without changing its position to prevent condensed liquid on its under-surface from running off on to the potatoes).

Shake the pan to make certain that the potato cake slides freely without sticking. Wipe the underside of the lid dry and, holding it firmly in place, turn it and the frying pan upside-down so that the potato cake rests on the lid, golden side up. Return the pan to the heat, add the remaining butter and tilt the lid to slide the cake back into the pan. Cook, uncovered, for about 15 minutes, then slip the cake on to a heated serving dish.

PEAR AND RED WINE ICE

INGREDIENTS
METRIC AND IMPERIAL

900 g (2 lb) firm, nearly ripe pears

200 g (7 oz) sugar

1 bottle of young, deeply coloured red wine

juice of ½ lemon

eau-de-vie de poire

Serves 4

Opposite: Pears for the Red Wine Ice

If preparing the ice in a *sorbetière* or ice cream maker, follow the manufacturer's instructions. If it is frozen in ice cube trays, it should be scraped out into a bowl when about two-thirds frozen, whisked briefly and returned to the trays to finish freezing. It may be prepared the previous day with no fear of its becoming too hard as the alcohol contained in the last addition of wine and in the eau-de-vie de poire (colourless, un-sweetened, distilled pear alcohol) will prevent it from freezing too firmly.

Halve or quarter the pears, core and peel them. Add the pears and sugar to a saucepan, pour over wine to cover and cook at a light boil until the pears are tender; depending on the variety, the time may vary from 15 to 20 minutes for nearly ripe eating pears to 1 hour or more for cooking pears. Drain the pears and return the liquid to the pan to reduce over medium heat.

Purée the pears in a food processor and transfer to a bowl. When the cooking liquid has reduced to the consistency of a light syrup, the boil rising up in a foam, stir it into the pear purée. Add some more red wine, a few drops of lemon juice and the eau-de-vie and taste for acidity; add more wine or lemon juice to bring the mixture to the desired level of sweet and acid balance.

Freeze the mixture when it has cooled. It is probably prettiest served in wine glasses.

DEPTH AND DELICACY FROM THE

The Loire river winds its way from the mountains of southern Auvergne, in the Ardêche, a stone's throw from Provence and the Rhône valley, up through the western part of the province of Burgundy and across the north-western half of France to its mouth at Nantes and the southern border of Brittany. It encompasses several regions and dozens of wines.

At the heart of France, halfway between the source and the mouth of the Loire, before it veers to the west, Sancerre and Pouilly Blanc Fumé (from Pouilly-sur-Loire, unrelated to Burgundy's Pouilly-Fuissé) are made from the Sauvignon grape, known in the region as *blanc fumé* because of the slightly smoky taste of the wines (Sancerre also makes a small amount of red from Pinot noir and the village of Pouilly-sur-Loire lends its name to a slight, thirst-quenching white made from the Chasselas grape). Sancerre and Pouilly Fumé are best drunk young in the full exultation of their fresh Sauvignon fruit.

At the mouth of the river, Muscadet and the two superior appellations, Muscadet de Sèvre-et-Maine (on the left bank) and Muscadet des Coteaux de la Loire (hugging both banks), are named after the grape variety, Muscadet, the local name for the Burgundian Melon grape, which was transplanted to the Nantais region in the seventeenth century. Muscadet's greatest charm is retained in the freshness of the year following the vintage. Like Sancerre and Pouilly Fumé, it washes down raw shellfish to perfection; none are particularly subtle wines but they are great fun to drink and all easily support the aggression of vinaigrettes and other sharp flavours.

Between these geographical extremes lie the vineyards of Touraine and Anjou where, except for a few of the lesser wines, the white Pineau de la Loire (Chenin blanc)

Apéritif: Muscadet de Sèvre-et-Maine (from the most recent
vintage) or Sancerre (young) or Pouilly Blanc Fumé
(young)

Stuffed Braised Squid Smothered in Little Peas
SAVENNIERES, CHATEAU D'EPIRE
1985

Roast Pork Loin Stuffed with Apricots,
Turnip Gratin
CHINON 'JEUNES VIGNES' CUVEE
DU CLOS DE LA CURE 1985
(or a young Saumur-Champigny)

Cheeses
SAINT-NICOLAS-DE-BOURGUEIL

Baked Pears
QUARTS-DE-CHAUME
(or Bonnezeaux 8–10 years old or more)

and the red Cabernet franc, locally known as Breton, reign supreme (Cabernet-Sauvignon is admitted but rarely planted). The vines of Vouvray, just east of Tours on the right bank, grow in chalky clay over limestone bedrock, which is riddled with labyrinthine cellars – former quarries from whose stones the old city of Tours was built – of an unvarying temperature and humidity in which these white wines evolve slowly and seem to remain fresh and lively forever. Whether they are very sweet (*liquoreux*), semi-sweet (*moelleux*) or dry, as most are today, they are firm wines, with a certain bite when young, which profit from a few years of age for the dry wines and many years for the sweeter wines, made from nobly rotted grapes (of those, my most moving memories are 1947s and 1959s). Because they have a natural tendency to sparkle, a proportion of the dry Vouvrays are rendered bubbly by the Champagne method.

Except for the region around Saumur and Champigny, bordering on the Touraine, of which it is a geological extension, the vineyard soils of the Anjou are mainly schistose and the most interesting wines are white. The wines of Savennières, on the right bank near Angers, in the past semi-sweet, are now nearly all dry. In *Les Vins de la Loire* (1956), Pierre Bréjoux describes the Château d'Epiré, placed on the following menu, as 'despairingly sweet'. Today, it is very dry with scents that nonetheless recall a sweeter past, a fine accompaniment to firm-flavoured fish – salmon, pike, red mullet, crustaceans, squid – or to poultry, simply roasted or in a cream sauce. To many people, Savennières is synonymous with the Clos de la Coulée de Serrant, a small vineyard resplendent with many centuries of history, upon which the present proprietor, Madame Joly, has lavished nearly 30 years of love. It shares with La Roche-aux-Moines the distinction of being able to incorporate the name of the growth into the official appellation (Appellation Savennières-Coulée de Serrant Contrôlée). Savennières needs a bit of age; depending on the vintage and the growth, somewhere between four and ten years is right (add a couple of years to each for la Coulée de Serrant).

Across the river, lying within the larger Coteaux du Layon region, are found two growths, Bonnezeaux and Quarts-de-Chaume, both on the right bank of the Layon river, which are endowed with microclimates especially encouraging to surmaturation, noble rot and the production of rich, liquorous, long-lived wines. In unusual years, the entire region produces lovely, semi-sweet or liquorous wines. During the sixties, at the Restaurant Prunier, rue Duphot, in Paris, I often drank an Anjou 1928, delicately sweet, floral and fresh, which today would be labelled Coteaux du Layon Rablay. I recently bought a few cases at auction – it is as fresh today as 25 years ago.

The Touraine red wines – Bourgueil and Saint-Nicolas-de-Bourgueil on the right bank, Chinon across the river and, adjoining Chinon across the border in Anjou, Saumur-Champigny – are the friendliest of wines: jubilant, frank and open, mingling herbal, grassy scents and flavours with an intense wild berry fruit which some define as raspberry, others as blackcurrant or bramble, and which may be simply the fruit of Cabernet franc. When drinking one of these wines, cool, on a hot day in the mottled shade of the grape arbour, I have only to close my eyes to recapture a child's summer-time sensation of lying face-down in the grass and cutting out the whole world except for vegetal and earthy scents and the lonely plaint of mourning doves in the silent air.

Why these wines should support the presence of sweet and savoury foods better than other red wines I would be hard put to explain, but so it seems to me. The last time I ate duck with orange was in November 1961 at a dinner in Paris, organised at the Restaurant Lasserre by *Cuisine et Vins de France*. The theme was '*Que Boire sur le Canard à l'Orange?*' Served with the duck were Champagne Henriot 1953, Anjou rosé de Cabernet 1955, Château-Chalon 1949, Beaujolais 1961, Saumur-Champigny 1959, Vieux Château Certan 1958 and Beaune 1er Cru Domaine de Saux 1957. The sauce was a heavily sugared mixture of orange juice and syrupy alcohols, bound by a slippery substance akin to cornflour; it demolished all the wines except for the Château-Chalon and the Champigny, both of which emerged from battle limping but intact.

Pork and prune preparations are traditional in Tourangelle cuisine; one of these wines is the ideal accompaniment, as they are also to a red wine stew of wild rabbit with a prune garnish. Depending on the style, they can be long-lived wines, but the lively fruit of a young wine seems best suited to foods of this bent. The lighter, faster maturing wines come from sandy and gravelly soils; those of a more severe structure from chalky, hillside soils with a higher clay content. The Chinon on this menu carries the mention '*jeunes vignes*' on the label, mainly as an indication that it is a wine best appreciated young; the vines are, in fact, fully mature – 15 years old and more – but the style is light, they grow in sandy soil and, to emphasise the precocious style, the pulp is macerated for a shorter time in the wine after fermentation, drawing fewer tannins into the finished wine. Drunk cool, within a year or two following the vintage, it is a ravishing summer wine.

TIMING

The roast will be stuffed and tied up ahead of time, ready to be put into the oven, the squid stuffed ahead of time, the shallots may be sweated in butter and held and the little peas shelled and kept fresh beneath a damp towel; the turnips may be grated, salted, squeezed and sweated in butter and the crumbs crisped in butter, ready to be assembled for the gratin.

About an hour and 20 minutes before going to table, put the pork roast in the oven; about 45 minutes before, put the squid to cook. The roast will be cooked and glazed when the squid are ready to serve; remove the roast, hold it in a warm place, and put the gratin in the oven just before going to table. The pears should be prepared at the last minute as they would discolour from oxidation if pre-prepared before being baked; the assemblage is, however, very simple and rapid and can easily be managed either during or after the cheese service while guests are relaxing with their last glass of red wine.

STUFFED BRAISED SQUID SMOTHERED IN LITTLE PEAS

Squid and cuttlefish respond in the same way to heat. Tiny and whole or, if larger, cut into rings, seared in a flash or plunged for a few seconds into boiling liquid, they are tender; left in contact with heat for a couple of minutes, they toughen and must, then, be exposed to a relatively long braising process to become tender again. Squid is the most practical of the two for stuffing because, in a cuttlefish, the section of the pouch wall from which the cuttlebone is removed is no more than a membrane, too easily torn.

A stuffing based on fresh breadcrumbs and a garlic persillade (page 15), pulled together with an egg or two, is also delicious; if the squid are not braised in tomato, one or two peeled, seeded and chopped tomatoes can be sautéed with the chopped shallots (or onion), tentacles and wings to be added to the stuffing. However the squid are to be braised, the dash of brandy and white wine is always valuable. Braised with a handful each of chopped onions and parsley and some chopped capers and anchovies (in salt, filleted and soaked) or with peeled, seeded and chopped tomatoes and aromatics (often called 'à l'américaine' because of its similarity to the lobster preparation of that name), they are wonderful, but better suited to a Mediterranean style of wine, white or rosé, than to the delicate Savennières. When braised with tomatoes, the sauce is usually too liquid and must be poured off and reduced before serving.

The peas should be picked while still tender enough to be eaten raw, before they turn starchy. Tender young broad beans, shelled and individually peeled, may be substituted (a branch of savory added) for the peas.

Squid are often sold already cleaned. If cleaning them yourself, first pull out the supple, isinglass-like spear that lies, loosely attached, the length of the inside body wall. Empty the pouch by pulling on the head; discard the soft innards that cling to it, tear the skin from the eyes and pull them out, holding the head under water to avoid spurting in case the eyes break, and press to either side of the orifice at the base of the tentacles to force out the beak. Tear the triangular wings, or fleshy fins, free from the pouch and rub off the fine, brownish-violet skin from both pouch and wings. Rinse well and put pouch, wings, head and tentacles to drain in a colander. When well drained, chop the wings, head and tentacles.

For the stuffing, parboil the rice in salted water for 12 to 15 minutes, then drain in a sieve and rinse with cold water. Leave to drain for 10 to 15 minutes.

Stew the chopped shallots in the butter, over low heat, until softened but uncoloured. Turn up the heat, throw in the chopped squid parts, season with salt, pepper and a suspicion of cayenne pepper and toss or stir until most of the liquid that the squid have given off has evaporated. Mix all of the elements of the stuffing together, delicately but intimately, tossing with a fork so as to crush no grain of rice.

INGREDIENTS
METRIC AND IMPERIAL

4 squid, body pouches 15–20 cm (6–8 in) long, cleaned

2–3 tbsp olive oil

about 2 tbsp brandy (Cognac, marc, fine, etc.)

about 4 tbsp white wine

225 g (8 oz) shallots

unsalted butter for cooking

900 g (2 lb) freshly picked little peas, shelled

salt

2 tbsp double cream

FOR THE STUFFING

150 g (5 oz) long-grain white rice

salt and freshly ground pepper

2–3 tbsp finely chopped shallots

15 g ($\frac{1}{2}$ oz) unsalted butter

cayenne pepper

1 tbsp finely chopped tender young winter savory leaves, or another herb to taste such as fines-herbes, fresh marjoram or thyme or a pinch of dried mixed herbs

Serves 4

Opposite: Stuffed, Braised Squid Smothered in Little Peas

Stuff the squid body pouches, using a teaspoon and forcing small quantities of stuffing at a time into the tip of the pouch, leaving no air pockets. Tack the tops of the pouches closed with a trussing needle and kitchen string, once through opposite sides, then again through the two other opposite sides, pulling the ends of the strings together, tying and clipping.

Over medium to high heat, in a sauté pan of a size to contain the stuffed squid at their ease, hardly touching, sauté them in the olive oil, shaking the pan and turning them around, until they shrink, turning more opaque and white and tightening themselves around the stuffing. Add the brandy, set it aflame and, when the flames have died, add the white wine. Cover tightly, adjust the heat to very low and braise gently for about 30 minutes, shaking the pan from time to time.

Meanwhile, peel the whole shallots and cook them gently, salted, in butter until semi-tender.

Add the shallots and peas to the stuffed squid with a sprinkle of salt, and continue braising, tightly covered, until the peas are of a melting tenderness, about 20 minutes longer. There should be very little liquid in the pan at this point – if it seems too abundant, strain it off into a small saucepan, reduce over high heat to about 3 tablespoons and pour it back over the squid and peas.

Just before serving, spoon over the cream and hold the pan, covered, for a minute, or the time necessary for the cream to melt into the juices, forming a light sauce. Serve directly from the sauté pan on to heated plates.

ROAST PORK LOIN STUFFED WITH APRICOTS

Your butcher will bone the loin. If you prefer to do it yourself, it is simply a question of beginning at the chine or bone end and separating both the loin and the tenderloin from the structure of T-bones, scraping against the bones and slitting the flesh free between the bones, leaving loin and tenderloin attached. Trim excess fat from the surface, leaving about 8 mm ($\frac{1}{3}$ in) thickness.

Macerate the dried apricots in the wine for several hours or overnight. Drain them and put the wine aside. Salt and pepper the inside of the boned loin and place the apricots in rows to either side of the tenderloin. Roll up the loin, tie it tightly with several rounds of kitchen string and salt and pepper the outside.

Preheat the oven to 180°–190°C (350°–375°F or Mark 4–5).

Roast the pork for about 45 minutes, then spoon off and discard all the clear fat that has collected in the roasting dish. Pour over part of the reserved maceration wine. Increase the oven heat to 230°C (450°F or Mark 8) and return the pork to cook for about 30 minutes, basting often and adding more macerating wine as needed (and, if it runs out, dribbles of more wine from the bottle or your glass), until the roast is a rich, glossy caramel colour on the surface.

Hold in a warm place until serving. Remove the strings with care so as not to destroy the effect of the glaze.

INGREDIENTS
METRIC AND IMPERIAL

1.4 kg (3 lb) pork loin, boned

100 g (4 oz) dried apricots

about 250 ml (8 fl oz) white wine

salt and freshly ground pepper

Serves 4

Roast Pork Loin Stuffed with Apricots, served with wine from Chinon

TURNIP GRATIN

INGREDIENTS
METRIC AND IMPERIAL

900 g (2 lb) small, crisp turnips

salt

unsalted butter

about 100 g (3½ oz) semi-fresh breadcrumbs

about 4 tbsp double cream

Serves 4

Similar gratins, very different in effect, can be made with practically any crisp vegetable that lends itself to grating, with some variations in treatment, depending on the demands of the individual vegetable. Swedes and courgettes, except that they are not peeled, can be treated in exactly the same way as the turnips; carrots are not salted but will profit by being first glazed, cooked with a dab of butter, a pinch each of sugar and salt and a little water, until all the water has evaporated, before being spread into the gratin dish with cream and crumbs and finished in the oven. I have never tried beetroot but don't doubt that an identical treatment, with a few drops of lemon juice added to the pre-cooking, would produce an attractive gratin. Potatoes should be rinsed but not salted, rolled tightly in a towel to dry them, sautéed with butter for a few seconds so that all are coated with a fine film, before being packed and smoothed into a gratin dish (no cream or crumbs necessary); sweet potatoes and celeriac may be treated in the same way as potatoes but need not be rinsed (celeriac, because of its penetrating flavour, may be preferred either mixed or layered with potatoes). Alternating layers of two different vegetables are amusing and, in the case of potatoes or a mixture of potatoes and celeriac, a handful of whole, peeled garlic cloves, tucked into the heart of the gratin between two layers of grated vegetables, will, after 45 minutes in a moderate oven, melt into a succulent pommade. A layer of sliced black truffles, in addition to the garlic, will break your heart for its sheer beauty.

Peel the turnips and grate them through the medium blade of a mouli-julienne or food processor. Layer them in a bowl, salting the layers. After 15 to 30 minutes squeeze the turnips free of excess liquid, then cook in a little butter over low heat for about 10 minutes.

Meanwhile, lightly colour the breadcrumbs in butter over very low heat.

Preheat the oven to 180°–190°C (350–375°F or Mark 4–5).

Spread the turnips in a gratin dish, spread over the cream thinly and sprinkle generously with the buttered crumbs. Bake for about 30 minutes, or until the surface is evenly golden.

Opposite: Baked Pears

BAKED PEARS

Halve the pears, remove the cores, peel and slice lengthwise. Preheat the oven to 200°C (400°F or Mark 6).

Butter a shallow gratin dish and spread the pear slices, overlapping fanwise, over the surface. Sprinkle with sugar, dab over cream and bake for 12 to 15 minutes, or until the cream is bubbling and the surface lightly coloured.

INGREDIENTS
METRIC AND IMPERIAL

4 firm eating pears

unsalted butter

2–3 tbsp sugar, or to taste

about 100 ml (3½ fl oz) double cream

Serves 4

Jura

The wines of the Jura are all unusual and, except for *vin jaune* and *vin de paille*, share a certain family resemblance – sturdy, muscular and friendly – whatever the colour.

The pink-fleshed and pale-skinned Poulsard grape is crushed and macerated with the skins for Pupillin rosé. Its allure, but for the colour, is that of a red wine; like more typical rosés, or light, simple, young and cool red wines or many rustic white wines, it is very much at home with sardines.

The most unusual of the Juras, perhaps of all French wines, is *vin jaune*, of which the best known bears the village appellation of Château-Chalon; made from the white Savignin grape, deeply coloured with bronze reflections, extraordinarily dry, concentrated, nutty in flavour and long-lived, it is often said to resemble sherry because, like fino sherries, it is kept for a long time (a minimum of six years), unracked and never topped up, in large kegs with the wine's surface protected from contact with air by a naturally formed film of yeasts. The analogy to sherry is superficial for *vin jaune* resembles only itself.

Best appreciated at a good cellar temperature (12°–14°C/about 55°F), *vin jaune* is good with seafood of pronounced flavours – lobster or salmon, for instance – and forms a surprising alliance with the rich flavours of duck, guinea fowl or game birds more often associated with red wines; it is also, in my experience, one of the few dry wines that can equably support the presence of sweet and savoury dishes, a privilege usually reserved for Sauternes or other white wines marked by noble rot.

Vin de paille, a sweet, gold-hued wine, so-called because in the past the grapes were dried on beds of straw before being pressed and fermented, is also from the Savignin grape. Today the grapes are hung on racks to dry. *Vin de paille* is no longer made commercially at Hermitage or in Burgundy, where it was once a tradition, and it is a rarity in the Jura. Vin Santo, from

BRAISED DUCK SERVED WITH
CHATEAU-CHALON

Apéritif: Côtes du Jura blanc or l'Etoile blanc

Stuffed Courgette Flowers
ARBOIS-PUPILLIN ROSE

Braised Stuffed Duck with Olives
CHATEAU-CHALON 1976
(or another vin jaune)

Cheeses
ARBOIS ROUGE

Souffléed Crêpes with Almonds and Sabayon Sauce
VIN DE PAILLE

---

various parts of Italy, is made in a similar way. A Gewürztraminer '*sélection de grains nobles*' from Alsace or a Sauternes will accompany equally well the souffléed crêpes.

TIMING

The duck is the only time-consuming preparation. It should be boned either the preceding day or early in the day for a dinner so that the stock may be put to cook for several hours to draw maximum flavour and gelatine from the carcass. Once stuffed, it will require a good two and a half hours in all for the initial roasting, the braising and the glazing processes. The stuffed courgette flowers can be put to cook just before the duck is returned to the oven for glazing; if the same oven is being used for both, the courgette flowers should be removed after ten minutes and kept, covered, in a warm place until serving. The crêpes may be prepared well in advance and, except for the final addition of beaten egg whites, the almond mixture can be prepared before the duck is put to cook. Prepare the Sabayon just before incorporating the egg whites into the almond mix.

STUFFED COURGETTE FLOWERS

Courgettes bear male and female flowers. It is the fruitless male flower which commonly serves in the kitchen (although it is now chic in modish restaurants to serve mousseline-stuffed female flowers with the tiny, just-formed vegetable attached). In Provence, as in Italy, they are always in the early morning, summer markets; the flowers fade rapidly and should be used very fresh but can be kept for several hours, the stem tips immersed in a glass of water and refrigerated. They are usually dipped in batter and deep-fried.

Instead of sardines, I often use fresh anchovies, which abound in all waters but which, outside France, apparently all go to the canning factories, for they are rarely seen on the market. Both have wonderfully delicate flesh which is perfectly thrown into relief by the light acidity of the sorrel, the Provençal whiff of garlic and olive oil and the indescribable, subtle flavour of the flowers, completely unlike that of courgettes. Both are very cheap and, for that reason, considered vulgar fare by French restaurant-goers. A few years ago, a young restaurateur friend asked me to help reorganise his menu and this preparation was amongst my suggestions. Not a single client ordered it in the space of a week's time so he substituted strips of salmon for the sardine fillets; it was an immediate success.

To fillet the sardines, cut off the heads, slit the length of the back with a small knife and pry each side free from the spinal bone with your fingertips. If the skin peels off easily, it will take the scales with it; if not, rinse under runnings water, rubbing gently to remove all scales. Trim the edges if any fin bones remain.

Fold each sorrel leaf lengthways, face inward, in one hand and pull the stem backward with the other hand to remove it. Rinse the leaves and drain.

Preheat the oven to 200°C (400°F or Mark 6).

Choose a gratin dish of a size just to contain the stuffed flowers, placed side by side in a single layer without packing. Mix together the sliced onion and garlic and spread half over the bottom of the dish. Season the sardine fillets, lay each along a sorrel leaf, roll it up and tuck the roll into a courgette flower, folding the petal tips inward to enclose it. Arrange on the bed of onion and garlic and sprinkle the remaining sliced onion and garlic over the surface. Dribble olive oil over the surface in a criss-cross pattern and sprinkle over the white wine. Cover with a sheet of foil and bake for about 10 minutes, then leave to rest, covered, in a warm place for another 10 or 15 minutes.

INGREDIENTS
METRIC AND IMPERIAL

8 fresh sardines

16 sorrel leaves

1 large onion, halved and thinly sliced

2 fresh garlic cloves, peeled and sliced paper-thin

salt and freshly ground pepper

16 courgette flowers, stems cut off at base

about 4 tbsp olive oil

about 100 ml (3 fl oz) white wine

Serves 4

Opposite: Stuffed Courgette Flowers

BRAISED STUFFED DUCK
WITH OLIVES

INGREDIENTS
METRIC AND IMPERIAL

1 duck, weighing about 1.8–2 kg
   (4–4½ lb)

olive oil

salt

coarse mirepoix (page 18), made
   with 2 carrots and 1 large onion

white wine

250 ml (8 fl oz) stock (page 18)
   made from neck and carcass
   chopped into pieces, wingtips
   and feet (blistered over a flame,
   skin rubbed off, rinsed)

100 g (4 oz) green olives in brine
   (picholine, if possible, not
   bottled)

few drops of lemon juice

FOR THE STUFFING

2 eggs

75–100 g (3–4 oz) ricotta cheese

1 garlic clove, peeled

pinch of coarse salt

large handful of fresh breadcrumbs

1 medium onion, finely chopped

few drops of olive oil or a bit of
   butter

duck heart, liver and fleshy lobes
   of gizzard, cut into small pieces

900 g (2 lb) Swiss chard, green
   parts only

about 1 tbsp finely chopped fresh
   marjoram

salt and freshly ground pepper

freshly grated nutmeg

Serves 4

Ten or twelve years ago, while I was visiting Simone (Simca) Beck, she produced two ducks and asked me to 'invent' something. The garden was full of chard, there was a remainder of brousse (ewe's milk ricotta) in the refrigerator and marjoram was growing outside the kitchen door; this was the inevitable result. The other guests were Julia and Paul Child and James Beard. Nothing remained at feast's end.

The ingredients and the quantities given for the stuffing here are flexible. Sometimes I eliminate the white cheese; if chard is not available, substitute spinach (but the rough, clean country taste of chard greens is an especially successful counterbalance to the suave, rich duck flavour); use the unopened flower buds of fresh (sweet, knotted) marjoram – if you have no fresh marjoram, substitute crumbled, dried oregano flowers or a healthy pinch of mixed dried herbs; the nutmeg is optional – if used, its presence should be so discreet as to be undetectable. When in season (January and February), the juice from a bitter Seville orange (bigarade) may be used to sharpen the sauce in place of lemon juice.

The size and shape of the cooking utensils are important. For the initial roasting and the final glazing process, a shallow, oval copper or enamelled ironware gratin dish of a size just to hold the duck is ideal. For the braising process, an oval cocotte into which the duck just fits, so as to be sufficiently immersed in a minimum of liquid, is essential (two ducks may be successfully braised in a large round pot).

The flesh of a duck is lean. Except for the loose fat inside the abdomen, which will be discarded before the bird is stuffed, all of the fat is in the skin structure; it will be drawn out and discarded during the cooking processes.

The neatest job of boning is done with a farm bird, ungutted, whose abdomen has not been cut into or, as in French markets, whose intestines have been removed without piercing the skin. Any gashes made by a butcher will have to be sewn up before the bird is stuffed. In France, I use Muscovy ducks (canards de Barbarie); farmed mallards are smaller than most domestic breeds (but, prepared in this way, one can easily serve four people). For flavour, they can't be beaten and they are less fat than others. Ducks from Chinese markets are more neatly butchered than most. Whatever is available will give good results.

If you receive the duck with feet attached, they will be a valuable addition to the stock. Cut out and discard the oil glands at the base of the tail to either side of the spinal column. Cut off the wingtips at the second joint, leaving only the shoulder joint attached to the body. If the bird has not been prepared by a butcher, remove the head, slit the neck skin down the back to the base of the neck, pull it free, along with the trachea and the oesophagus, cut halfway through the neck where it joins the body and twist it off. Pull the oesophagus, crop and trachea free from the neck skin and pull them out.

Boning is easy; it takes 10 minutes to bone a duck, but I have now spent a frustrating week trying, unsuccessfully, to make it sound as simple as it really is. The fact is that clinical descriptions of boning are interminable, boring and intimidating and that, however precise the instructions may be, you will still have to feel your way with prodding fingertips and the point of a small, sharp knife. You should know, however, that before the flesh and skin can be peeled free of the carcass, the wishbone must be removed and the shoulder blades and the collar bones, which are attached, must be severed from the shoulder joint and removed. The shoulder blades are free-floating in the flesh of the back and can be pulled out through pinched thumb and forefinger; the collar bones are connected to the breastbone by tender cartilage and are easily snapped free. When you arrive at the leg level, bend the legs backward to rupture partially the connection of the thigh bones to the ball sockets before severing the connection with the knife tip. When the bird is completely turned inside-out, cut through the backbone at the base of the tail, leaving the last, tiny vertebrae in the tail.

The liver, gizzard and heart will be used in the stuffing. Take care to remove a fragment of liver with the gall bladder when cutting it free to make certain that it neither breaks nor leaks any bitter fluid. Cut the fleshy lobes of the gizzard free from the gristly, tough inner skin.

To make the stuffing, mash the eggs with the ricotta to loosen it up. Pound the garlic to a paste with the salt in a mortar. Wipe the garlic out of the mortar with the breadcrumbs and add to the ricotta. Cook the onion over low heat in the oil or butter until softened but not coloured. Add the pieces of heart, liver and gizzard a minute before removing from the heat, then tip into the cheese mixture.

Parboil the chard for less than a minute, drain and refresh under cold running water. Squeeze well and chop, then add to the cheese mixture along with the remaining ingredients for the stuffing. Mix thoroughly with your hands. Taste for salt.

Preheat the oven to 230°C (450°F or Mark 8).

Fill the bird loosely with the mixture (during cooking, the stuffing swells and the flesh contracts; if packed, the bird will burst). Turn the duck over, back facing up, and fold the neck flap over the back. To truss, use a trussing needle at least 15 cm (6 in) long and two lengths of kitchen string, each about 75 cm (30 in) long. Run the first length of string through the upper part of each shoulder, at the same time pinning the neck flap to the body. Turn the duck on to its back, pull the legs into place and run the needle through the top end of the drumsticks, near the thigh joints and through the body. Tie the string ends together without pulling too tightly and clip off the excess. Repeat with the other length of string, this time piercing the lower end of each wing joint, while pinning the end of the neck flap to the body, and the lower end of each drumstick, again running the needle through the body and tying as before.

Rub the surface of the duck with a few drops of olive oil,

Braised, Stuffed Duck with Olives, with Château-Chalon from the Jura region

sprinkle with salt and wrap the bone tip of each drumstick with a fragment of foil to prevent its burning. Roast for 30 to 40 minutes, basting regularly with the fat after about 15 minutes; this both helps draw out more fat and encourages even browning.

Spread the mirepoix in the bottom of the cocotte and place the duck on top. Remove the foil wrappings. Discard all the fat in the roasting dish, deglaze with white wine and pour the juices over the duck. Add the stock and pour over enough white wine to immerse the duck by about three-quarters. Bring to a near boil, adjust the heat to maintain a bare simmer and cook, covered, for about 1¼ hours. Use an asbestos pad or other heat disperser, if necessary, to prevent the braising juices from arriving at a boil.

While the duck is simmering, parboil the olives for a few minutes and drain. Set aside.

Return the duck to its roasting dish. Pour the braising juices through a fine sieve into a small saucepan, pressing the mirepoix to extract all juices. Discard the mirepoix. When the fat rises to the surface of the braising liquid, remove as much as possible. Bring the liquid to a near boil, then move the pan half off the heat to maintain a light boil to one side of the surface while a skin of fatty sediment forms to the other side. Lift a couple of ladles of liquid from the boiling side, pour them over the duck and put the roasting dish into the oven set at 190°–200°C (375°–400°F or Mark 5–6). From this point on, the duck should be basted regularly, with another ladle of fatless sauce being poured over from time to time as the juices in the roasting dish disappear. At the same time, the sauce in the saucepan should be regularly cleansed, the skin forming to the still side of the surface being pulled to the edge with the side of a tablespoon and removed. When practically no more fat is being drawn out of the sauce, add the parboiled olives and simmer for a few minutes. When the duck is coated in a glossy, deep caramel-coloured glaze, it is ready.

To remove the strings, clip to one side of the knot and pull on the knot, steadying the bird with the back of a fork. Transfer the duck to a heated platter. Pour any liquid from the roasting dish into the saucepan and deglaze the roasting dish with a little white wine, scraping sides and bottom with a wooden spoon to dissolve all solidified juices. Lift the olives out of the sauce with a perforated spoon, scatter them around the duck and pour the deglazing juices into the saucepan. Skim again, sharpen the sauce with a little lemon juice (or bitter orange juice) and finally pass it through a small sieve into a sauceboat.

To carve the duck, first remove each wing with a section of breast and stuffing, cutting down at a bias to avoid touching the bone. Slice the body crosswise into slices until you reach the legs. Slice off each leg with a portion of stuffing and finish slicing crosswise the section of body left between the legs.

SOUFFLEED CREPES WITH ALMONDS

AND SABAYON SAUCE

INGREDIENTS
METRIC AND IMPERIAL

FOR THE CREPES

1 egg

1 heaped tbsp flour

pinch of salt

about 80 ml (3 fl oz) milk

1 tbsp Cognac, Armagnac, etc.

15 g (½ oz) unsalted butter,
melted in the crêpe pan

FOR THE FILLING

200 g (7 oz) shelled almonds,
peeled (page 20)

4–5 bitter almonds, peeled
(page 20), or few drops of
almond essence

small pinch of salt

65 g (2½ oz) sugar

3 eggs, separated

80 ml (3 fl oz) white wine

TO SERVE

Sabayon sauce (page 21)

Serves 4

As you make the crêpes, stack them in a pile on a plate to prevent their drying out. If made ahead of time, cover the plate with plastic film. If they have been refrigerated, they may stick together because of the butter contained in them but it is only necessary to place them for a few moments in a warm oven or over hot water to separate them. Specific proportions are less important than the consistency of the batter, but a high proportion of egg and a low proportion of flour will make the most tender crêpes. The following one-egg recipe will make 10 or 12 small crêpes (pan measuring 12 cm/5 in bottom diameter) if the batter is sufficiently thin. Use a small ladle (4 tablespoon capacity) about half filled with batter for pouring.

The almond mixture is too heavy to rise as high as a traditional soufflé but it is delicious and, if it does not rise as high, neither does it fall as fast.

(I once demonstrated a similar preparation, in the form of a soufflé pudding, to the Tulsa Ladies' Club. The ingredients had been measured out in advance and neatly ordered on a tray to permit me to babble at ease without thinking about what I was doing. When the thing came out of the oven, it was glorious to behold. Portions were passed out and it was only when the ladies began to make polite observations to the tune of, 'how very interesting', 'very unusual', 'extraordinary', that I stuck my finger into a bowl of what I had assumed to be salt and tasted the sugar that should have gone into the pudding mix . . . I did not taste the salt soufflé.)

To make the crêpes, add the egg to the flour and salt and whisk from the centre of the bowl, moving outward and gradually adding most of the milk, until all the flour is absorbed. Whisk in the brandy and the melted butter. Add more milk if necessary to bring the batter to the consistency of fresh, fluid cream; if there are any lumps, pass it first through a sieve before using.

Wipe the crêpe pan with a paper towel, leaving only a film of butter (the pan will not be buttered in between crêpes – the batter contains enough butter to prevent their sticking). Heat the pan over medium to low heat. Remove from the heat and give the pan a rotating, undulating motion as you pour in the batter so as just to coat the bottom without excess. The batter should sizzle on contact. Return the pan to the heat and, when the edges of the crêpe turn golden and begin to curl free from the pan's surface, slip a small spatula or a round-tipped table knife beneath to flip it over. After a few seconds slip the crêpe from the pan with your fingertips. Remove the pan from the heat for a few seconds between each crêpe to prevent its becoming overheated, and give the batter a stir each time before ladling it out. The first side cooked is always the most evenly coloured and the most attractive and should always be presented as the outside surface of a parcel, roll or folded crêpe.

For the filling, add the ingredients progressively to a food processor, first the almonds, then the salt, sugar, egg yolks and wine. Whir to a fairly fine purée; the texture will remain granular. Remove to a mixing bowl. Whisk the egg whites to soft peaks (if not using a copper bowl, you may prefer to add the pinch of salt to the egg whites instead of to the almond mixture). Fold about one-third of the whites quite evenly into the almond mix, then add the remainder and fold in delicately without insisting on a homogeneous incorporation.

Preheat the oven to 200°C (400°F or Mark 6).

Hold each crêpe, second cooked side facing up, on the palm of your hand, place a heaped tablespoon of the filling in the middle and place on a baking tray, folded slightly less than half over the filling so that the under lip of the crêpe protrudes and the mounded filling is visible. Bake for about 4½ minutes or a few seconds longer, until the edges of the crêpes are crisp and deep golden brown and the body swelled. Serve immediately on warmed plates, accompanied by the Sabayon sauce.

Souffléed Crêpes with Almonds and Sabayon Sauce

THE ELEGANCE OF

Except for Edelzwicker, a light, refreshing wine with a discernible sparkle, made from a mixture of local grape varieties, most of whose diminishing production is dispensed in Alsatian brasseries by the pitcher in the year following the vintage, the wines of Alsace are made from single grape varieties: Sylvaner, Pinot blanc, Riesling, Tokay-Pinot gris, Gewürztraminer Muscat d'Alsace and Pinot noir. It is white wine country; Pinot noir, the only red variety, from which vin rosé and very light-coloured, sometimes greyish, reds are made, is raised mostly for the form. Sylvaner and Pinot blanc, good apéritif, charcuterie and hors d'oeuvre wines, have a less pronounced varietal character than the other Alsatian white varieties.

Since 1975, certain hillside terrains, distinguished by privileged expositions and soil compositions and with a tradition of producing superior wines, have been granted the right to the appellation Alsace Grand Cru. To enjoy this appellation, only Riesling, Tokay-Pinot gris, Muscat d'Alsace or Gewürztraminer may be grown there.

Riesling is the classic noble grape of Alsace. Its wines are typically steely and lean, more skeleton than flesh, with finesse and elegance – all banal, abstract terms that come to life in the glass and in the mouth. Tokay-Pinot gris wines have more muscle but, perhaps, less breeding.

Because the penetrating fruit of Muscat is felt to be incompatible with food, Muscat d'Alsace is usually served as an apéritif wine. On a recent trip to Alsace, organised for l'Académie Internationale du Vin, Jean Meyer (Jos. Meyer & Fils, Wintzenheim) served his Muscat 1986 at lunch, first with asparagus and, later, with the cheese course, a farm Münster, both times with great success. In emulation, I have placed a Muscat d'Alsace on the cheeses in the following menu; it may be difficult to find a good Alsatian Münster but the Muscat will support other high-scented, soft-ripened cheeses, as well as blue cheeses, both

PEACH AND BREAD PUDDING WITH
SABAYON SAUCE

of which are troublesome in the presence of fine red wines.

Until this trip, I had never tasted a Gewürztraminer *sélection de grains nobles*, made from individually picked grapes, withered either by noble rot or by simple desiccation. To my palate, the sweet and spicy, floral perfume of Gewürztraminer has never seemed to fit a dry wine and even the *vendange tardive* or late harvest Gewürztraminers, with an edge of sweetness, rarely seem to come together. But all preconceptions and prejudices vanished with the Gewürztraminers *sélection de grains nobles* that we tasted in the cellars of Trimbach, Hugel and Léon Beyer, all sumptuous and liquorous wines in beautiful balance; I was hopelessly seduced, Gewürztraminer is one of the most interesting of wines for the confection of a Sabayon sauce; in that role, a dry version, much less expensive than *vendange tardive* or *sélection de grains nobles*, serves well.

TIMING

Prepare the noodle dough, roll it out and cut it before putting the rabbit to work. The pudding may be baked before or at the same time as the rabbit. Pare and slice the artichokes after the rabbit goes in the oven; they and the fish only require a few minutes for cooking and assemblage. The noodles are cooked in a couple of minutes. The Sabayon sauce may be prepared at the last minute.

PERSILLADE OF SOLE
AND SLICED ARTICHOKES

Cut each sole fillet on the bias into strips aproximately 1 cm (⅓ in) wide. Melt the butter in a pan over low heat, add the strips of sole fillet and season with salt and pepper. Shake the pan gently, stirring and turning the strips around with a wooden spoon, until they begin to turn opaque and firmer to the touch – no more than 1 minute if they are not too crowded in the pan. Remove from the heat and hold them in their pan while preparing the artichokes.

Halve the artichoke bottoms and slice them as thinly as possible. Toss immediately in lemon juice to prevent discoloration, then drain and dry in a towel. Heat the oil in a large frying pan, over high heat. Add the sliced artichoke bottoms, salt and pepper and shake and toss every few seconds for a couple of minutes or until the slices begin to curl and turn golden at the edges. Throw in the persillade, toss a couple of times, add the strips of sole, toss again for a few seconds and serve on to warm plates.

INGREDIENTS
METRIC AND IMPERIAL

2 large soles, filleted (8 fillets)
about 25 g (1 oz) unsalted butter
salt and freshly ground pepper
2–3 medium to large raw artichoke bottoms (page 20)
lemon juice
about 3 tbsp olive oil
persillade (page 15)

Serves 4

Persillade of Sole and Sliced Artichokes

BAKED RABBIT IN SAFFRON CREAM

INGREDIENTS
METRIC AND IMPERIAL

1 rabbit, cut up as for a sauté, head split in two, liver and heart reserved

salt

finely chopped fresh marjoram or mixed dried herbs

fragment of unsalted butter

FOR THE BASTING MIXTURE

pinch of cayenne pepper

knife-tip of powdered saffron, or a pinch of saffron threads, or both, dissolved in a few drops of boiling water

2 tbsp, more or less, Dijon mustard

juice of 1 lemon

2–3 tbsp white wine

250 ml (8 fl oz) double cream

FOR THE GARNISH

1 red pepper, split, cored, seeded and cut into thin strips

salt

15 g (½ oz) butter

handful of spring onions, thinly sliced

Serves 4

The one-step principle (assemble, bake, baste and serve) is the only constant of this dish. Sometimes I eliminate the saffron. The garnish varies with the seasons: in spring, tiny peas or podded and peeled broad beans, parboiled for a few seconds; at the height of summer, garden tomatoes, peeled, seeded, cut into pieces and sautéed for a minute in a bit of olive oil over high heat, torn-up basil added halfway; in another menu context, quartered, butter-stewed artichoke hearts, alone or in combination with one of the preceding garnishes.

Amongst possible variations on the theme, I have noted: rabbit pieces coated with a mixture of finely chopped onion, celery, garlic, parsley and prosciutto fat, mixed herbs and salt, packed into oven casserole, remaining mixture scattered over, split, cored chicory cut into thin strips and spread over, baked tightly covered for an hour, a few spoons of salted cream, mustard and lemon juice mixture dabbed across the surface, baked again, uncovered, for 15 minutes; rabbit pieces marinated with mixed herbs, bay, sliced onions and a bit of white wine, layered with the onions, peeled small potatoes, a head of peeled new garlic cloves, salted, covered with a chiffonade of sorrel, mixture of cream, mustard, lemon juice and marinade spooned over, baked . . .

Preheat the oven to 180°–190°C (350–375°F or Mark 4–5).

Lay the rabbit pieces out on a chopping board or platter and sprinkle all surfaces with salt and the herb or herbs of your choice.

For the basting mixture, whisk together the spices, mustard, lemon juice and wine, then whisk in the cream. Dip the rabbit pieces in the mixture and transfer to an oven dish in which they may be arranged in a single layer. Spoon over a bit more of the mixture and hold the rest for basting. Bake for about 1 hour, beginning to baste with the mixture held in reserve after 15 to 20 minutes. Don't drown the rabbit; as long as there is enough sauce in the oven dish, use it for basting before adding more.

Meanwhile, prepare the garnish. Cook the pepper strips, salted, in the butter over low heat, covered, until nearly tender but not coloured, shaking or stirring occasionally. Just before removing from the heat, stir in the sliced spring onions. About 10 minutes before removing the rabbit from the oven, scatter the pepper and onions over the surface. Baste the garnish a couple of times before removing from the oven.

At the last minute, melt a small amount of butter in a small pan, add the heart and liver, cut into small pieces or thinly sliced, season and stir around over medium heat for a few seconds, only long enough to turn the surfaces greyish and to firm up the flesh. Scatter over the rabbit just before serving.

FRESH NOODLES

As a garnish, noodles are more manageable cut into short, 10–15 cm (4–6 in) lengths than left long. If using a pasta machine, cut the rolled-out strips of dough into short lengths before passing them through the cutters; if rolled out and cut by hand, cut them first, then spread out the unrolled lengths and cut through them to shorten them.

Put about two-thirds of the flour into a mixing bowl. Add the salt, oil and eggs and mix with a fork, adding more flour as needed to form a dough. Knead, sprinkling with flour, until the dough is quite firm but sufficiently supple to be easily rolled out. Cover with a towel and leave to rest for at least 30 minutes.

If using a machine, separate the dough into two portions. Flatten one on a floured surface with the palm of your hand and roll it slowly through the kneading rollers at their widest setting. Press again on the floured surface, fold and pass again through the rollers. Repeat, folding in three. Don't pass it through the rollers any more times than necessary to bring it together into a consistent, non-crumbly sheet of pasta. Pass it two or three times between the rollers, each time adjusted to a finer thickness, the last time through the next to finest adjustment. Hang to dry (over a broomstick propped between two chairbacks) for 20 minutes or so before passing through the cutters and tossing lightly with a bit of flour to prevent the noodles sticking together.

Alternatively, roll out thinly by hand and hang to dry. Lay the sheet of pasta back on the work surface, sprinkle with a bit of semolina or fine cornmeal to discourage sticking and roll the sheet of pasta up, loosely, from either side so that the rolls meet in the middle. Slice into noodles with a chef's knife; to unroll them, slip the blade of the knife flatly beneath, the back of the blade to the centre, and lift up so that the noodles unroll to either side of the blade.

Cook in a large pot of boiling salted water. Fresh noodles require no more than a couple of minutes' cooking; test a noodle between finger and thumbnail for doneness. Drain and toss in the butter at the moment of serving.

INGREDIENTS
METRIC AND IMPERIAL

225 g (8 oz) strong bread flour

salt

1 tbsp olive oil

3 eggs

about 40 g (1½ oz) unsalted butter, diced

Serves 4

Opposite: Rabbit pieces dipped in the Saffron Cream mixture before cooking

PEACH AND BREAD PUDDING

WITH SABAYON SAUCE

INGREDIENTS
METRIC AND IMPERIAL

75 g (3 oz) unsalted butter

about 150 g (5 oz) semi-dry country bread, torn into pieces

handful of raisins, macerated for several hours in a bit of kirsch or other eau-de-vie

3–4 ripe peaches, peeled and sliced

4 tbsp sugar, or more to taste

3 eggs

500 ml (18 fl oz) milk and cream mixed, half and half

TO SERVE

Sabayon sauce (page 21), made with Gewürztraminer

Serves 4

Preheat the oven to 180°–190°C (350°–375°F or Mark 4–5).

Melt half the butter in a large frying pan and cook the bread pieces over low heat, adding more butter as necessary and tossing or stirring and turning until they are lightly golden and the surfaces are crisp. Empty into a buttered gratin dish. Scatter over the raisins and peach slices, tucking them in here and there and arranging with the pieces of bread to form a fairly regular surface.

Whisk together the sugar and eggs and whisk in the milk and cream. Pour evenly over the contents of the gratin dish. Bake for about 40 minutes or until the custard is set. Serve tepid, accompanied by the Sabayon sauce.

ACKNOWLEDGEMENTS

PICTURE CREDITS

The photographs in this book were taken at the author's house in the South of France by Bob Komar, assisted by Kim Golding.

The artwork illustrations are by Sarah McMenemy.

ACKNOWLEDGEMENTS

The editors would like to thank:

Sylvia Celentano, Valerie Chandler, Kathryn Cureton, Joanna Edwards, Katherine Judge, Antony Mason, Rob Mitchell, Christine Noble, Helen Seccombe, Nancy Webber.

INDEX

Note: Page numbers in italics refer to *further mentions* of the recipes; bold numbers refer to illustrations.

A

Almonds: standard preparation 20
  Almond Bavarian cream and peaches in Sauternes 79, 84, **85**
  Souffléed crêpes with almonds and Sabayon sauce 7–8, *112*, *118–9*, **119**
Anchovies *113*
Apples: Honey-glazed apple tart 72, **73**
Apricots: Roast pork loin stuffed with apricots *103–4*, 107, **107**
Aromatics *13–18*
Artichokes *69*, *124*; standard preparation 20
  Braised artichoke bottoms with glazed onions 27, 31
  Persillade of sole and sliced artichoke *122*, 123, **123**
Asparagus 27, *120*
  Scrambled eggs with asparagus 27, 28–9, **29**
Aubergine *90*

B

Bacon
  Brochettes of scallops, monkfish and bacon *90*, *91*, 94, **95**
Beans, Broad *61*, *68–9*, *105*, *124*
Beans, Green *68*; salad *7*
  Green beans (recipe) 83
  Pilaf with spring vegetables *58*, 61
Beef 27, *70*
  Roast beef **25**, **26**, 27, 30–1
Braised artichoke bottoms with glazed onions 27, 31
Braised chicory *67*, *68–9*, **68**
Braised stuffed duck with olives *47*, **111**, *112*, 114–7, **115**, **116**
Bread: with *farce gratin* 97

Peach and bread pudding with Sabayon sauce 121, *122*, 126
Bream *58*
Brochettes of lamb parts in caul **55**, *58*, 60, **61**
Brochettes of scallops, monkfish and bacon *90*, *91*, 94, **95**

C

Cabbage: Pig's trotters and cabbage braised in Beaujolais *37*, 42, **42**
Carrots *18*, *108*
  Pilaf with spring vegetables *58*, 61
Celeriac *108*
  White purée **45**, *47*, **51**, 52
Celery heart *61*
Chard, Swiss
  Braised stuffed duck with olives *47*, **111**, *112*, 114–7, **115**, **116**
Cheese **32**, **55**, **62**, *67*, *78*, *120–2*
  In recipes 38–9, 59, 114–7
Chicken 27, *70*, *102*
Courgette flowers, Stuffed *112*, **112**, 113
Courgettes *68–9*, *108*
  Courgette and tomato tart *58*, 59, **59**
Crêpes: see Souffléed crêpes
Crépinettes: Oysters and green sausages 79, 80, **81**
Cuttlefish *105*

D

Duck *102*, *103*, *110*
  Braised stuffed duck with olives *47*, **111**, *112*, 114–7, **116**
Duck terrine **87**, *91*, 92–3

E

Eggs *18*, 27
  Scrambled eggs with asparagus 27, 28–9, **29**
Elvers *94*

F

Farce gratin 97
Figs *69*
  Gratin of fresh figs *58*, 63, **63**
Fish *57*, *58*, *102*, *110*; see also individual species
Flowers, as food 6, 7
  Stuffed courgette flowers *112*, **112**, 113
Foie gras *78*
Fruits, Mixed
  Macedoine of fruits in Beaujolais *37*, 43, **43**

G

Game *47*, *70*, *92*, *96*, *110*; see also Pheasant; Rabbit
Garlic *69*; in persillade *15–16*; vinaigrette *18*
Gratin of fresh figs *58*, 63, **63**
Green salad, Tossed 7, **8**, *17*

H

Herbs *14–16*, *17*
Honey-glazed apple tart 72, **73**
Honey ice cream 33, **33**

I

Ice: Pear and red wine ice *91*, 98, **99**
Ice cream, Honey 33, **33**

L

Lamb *70*, *90*
  Brochettes of lamb parts in caul **55**, *58*, 60, **61**
  Leg of lamb on a bed of potatoes 79, 82–3, **82**
  Stuffed, braised lam shoulder **45**, *47*, 50–1, **51**
Lettuce *17*, *69*

M

Macedoine of fruits in Beaujolais 37, 43, **43**
Marinade **16**
Marjoram *14–15*
Mirepoix of vegetables 18
Monkfish: Brochettes of scallops, monkfish and bacon *90, 91,* 94, **95**
Mussels: Seafood salad with saffron cream sauce *47, 48–9,* **49**

N

Noodles, Fresh *122,* 125

O

Olives: Braised stuffed duck with olives *47,* **111,** *112,* 114–7, **115, 116**
Onions *6, 69, 70*
    Braised artichoke bottoms with glazed onions 27, 31
    Stuffed onions baked in cream sauce 37, 38–9, **39**
    White purée **45,** *47,* **51,** 52
Oxtail and pig's ear stew **16,** *47,* **65,** *67, 70–1,* **71**
Oysters and green sausages *79,* 80, **81**

P

Parsley *14, 15–16, 17,* 18
Pastry: standard preparation 20–21
    In recipes 59, 72
Peaches *43*
    Almond Bavarian cream and peaches in Sauternes *79,* 84, **85**
    Peach and bread pudding with Sabayon sauce **121,** *122,* 126
    Peaches in red Crozes-Hermitage *47,* 53, **53**
Pears *43*
    Baked pears *104,* 109, **109**
    Pear and red wine ice *91,* 98, **99**
Peas *61, 68–9, 124*
    Stuffed braised squid smothered in little peas 7, **101,** *103,* **104,** **104,** 105–6
Persillade *15–16*
Persillade of sole and sliced artichoke *122,* 123, **123**
Pheasant *92*
    Roast pheasant *91,* 96–7, **97**
Pig's trotters and cabbage braised in Beaujolais 37, 42, **42**

Pilaf with spring vegetables *58,* 61
Pistachios: standard preparation 20
    In recipes *40–1,* 84
Pork *70*
    Roast pork loin stuffed with apricots *103–4,* 107, **107**
    see also Sausage meat
Potatoes *108*
    Leg of lamb on a bed of potatoes *79,* 82–3, **82**
    Potato straw cake *91,* 98
    White purée **45,** *47,* **51,** 52
Poultry *27, 70, 102; see also* Duck
Prosciutto
    Braised chicory *67, 68–9,* **68**
    Duck terrine **87,** *91,* 92–3

R

Rabbit *70, 92, 103*
    Baked rabbit in saffron cream *122,* 124, **124**
Raspberry sauce *33;* standard preparation 21
Rice
    Pilaf with spring vegetables *58,* 61
    Stuffed braised squid smothered in little peas 7, **101,** *103,* **104,** **104,** 105–6

S

Sabayon sauce: standard preparation 21
    In recipes 118–9, 126
Saffron
    Baked rabbit in saffron cream *122,* 124, **124**
    Seafood salad with saffron cream sauce *47, 48–9,* **49**
Salads *6–7,* **8,** *17, 18, 69*
Salmon *94, 102, 110, 113*
Sausage meat: standard preparation 19
    In recipes *40–1,* 80, *92–3*
Scallops
    Brochettes of scallops, monkfish and bacon *90, 91,* 94, **95**
Seafood salad with saffron cream sauce *47, 48–9,* **49**
Sole *48*
    Persillade of sole and sliced artichoke *122,* 123, **123**
Souffléed crêpes with almonds and Sabayon sauce *7–8,* **112,** 118–9, **119**

Squid *102*
    Seafood salad with saffron cream sauce 7, *47, 48–9,* **49**
    Stuffed braised squid smothered in little peas 7, **101,** *103,* **104,** 105–6
Stock: standard preparation 18
Sweetbreads: Veal sweetbreads sweated in Sauternes **75,** *78, 79,* 82

T

Terrine: Duck terrine **87,** *91,* 92–3
Tomatoes *61, 90, 124;* salad *6–7*
    Courgette and tomato tart *58, 59,* **59**
    Stuffed onions baked in cream sauce 37, 38–9, **39**
Truffles *108*
    Duck terrine **87,** *91,* 92–3
    Truffled sausage with pistachios in court-bouillon **35,** *36–7, 40–1,* **41**
Turnips
    Turnip gratin *103,* 104, 108
    White purée **45,** *47,* **51,** 52

V

Veal sweetbreads sweated in Sauternes **75,** *78, 79,* 82
Vegetable(s) *6, 67;* braised *68–9;* gratin *108;* mirepoix 18; purée *52; see also* individual species
Vinaigrette *17–18*
Vinegar *6, 16–18*

W

White purée **45,** *47,* **51,** 52
Wines: choosing **8, 9;** care, serving *9–10, 12–13;* tasting *10;* French wine classifications *10–12;* Alsace *120–2;* Bordeaux *10, 11–12,* Northern Bordeaux *86–91,* Southern Bordeaux *74–9;* Burgundy: Northern Burgundy *11, 12, 24–7,* Southern Burgundy *34–7;* Champagne *9, 10,* Côtes du Rhône *44–7;* Jura *110–12;* Loire *100–03;* Provence *54–7;* South West France *64–7*